DON'T FORGET THE DUCT TAPE

SECOND EDITION

**TIPS & TRICKS
FOR REPAIRING
& MAINTAINING
OUTDOOR &
TRAVEL GEAR**

Kristin Hostetter

THE MOUNTAINEERS BOOKS

THE MOUNTAINEERS BOOKS
is the nonprofit publishing arm of The Mountaineers, an
organization founded in 1906 and dedicated to the exploration,
preservation, and enjoyment of outdoor and wilderness areas.

1001 SW Klickitat Way, Suite 201, Seattle, WA 98134

© 2007 by Kristin Hostetter

First edition, 2003. Second edition: first printing 2007, second printing 2008, third printing 2009, fourth printing 2011, fifth printing 2015

Manufactured in the United States of America

Acquiring Editor: Laura Drury
Project Editor: Annabel A. Cassam
Copy Editor: Carol Poole
Cover Design: Mayumi Thompson
Text Design and Layout: Marge Mueller, Gray Mouse Graphics
Illustrations: Moore Creative Designs and Gray Mouse Graphics

Library of Congress Cataloging-in-Publication Data
Hostetter, Kristin.
  Don't forget the duct tape / Kristin Hostetter. — 2nd ed.
      p. cm.
  Includes bibliographical references and index.
  ISBN 0-89886-955-2 (paperbound : alk. paper)
1. Outdoor recreation—Equipment and supplies—Maintenance and repair. I. Title.
    GV191.76.H67 2007
    796.5—dc22

                                                2006037849

 Printed on recycled paper
ISBN (paperback):978-0-89886-955-2
ISBN (ebook): 978-1-59485-117-9

For Charlie and Joey,
everything's for you.

CONTENTS

FOREWORD

Maybe, like me, you're a clumsy camper. Maybe you break things, too. Trekking poles. Tent zippers. Sunglasses, stoves, stakes, and so on. Or perhaps you're just one of those hard-driving hikers who thrash their gear because—hey, that's what it was built for, and the outdoors is a rough-and-tumble place. Either way, you've picked up the right book. This handy little repair manual is the perfect pocket reference for every outdoor enthusiast who's ever poked a hole in a pair of Gore-Tex gaiters and not known how to patch it up.

Ten years ago, on my very first hike with Kristin, she showed the fix-it ingenuity that fills the pages of *Don't Forget the Duct Tape*. There were six of us on a weeklong hike on the Appalachian Trail and other paths in New York's Harriman State Park. We were testing external-frame packs, a breed that's now nearly extinct yet has always been known for its durability. Except on this trip. We encountered one problem after another, including a failure our veteran group had never seen when the top sheared off a clevis pin. Those of you who've carried external-frame packs are grimacing in sympathy right now—these bolt-like devices connect the pack bag to the frame. Without them, the pack doesn't work.

While the rest of us sat scratching our heads, Kristin—who'd been a pack-fitter and outdoor store employee before becoming *Backpacker*'s gear editor—dug into her load with the sly grin of a gourmet chef who's just realized the perfect ingredient for her new soufflé recipe. Out came her car keys and Leatherman multitool. One key ring and some artful pliers work followed, and in five minutes we were moving again.

In the years since that fast fix, Kristin and I have tested

more than a thousand products for *Backpacker*, and we've spent nearly that many days on the trail. She's seen it all in that time, from shattered tent poles to moldy boots to—just a few months ago—a new stove that spewed white gas on us from two different leaks. With each misfire, her arsenal of repair tricks gets deeper, which is part of the reason she's penned this second, expanded edition of *Duct Tape*.

Whether you're carrying a well-stocked repair kit or traveling superlight, Kristin has a DIY method for almost every gear breakdown you can imagine. She also dispenses wisdom for maintaining your equipment back at home—Chapter 1 alone, on cleaning and restoring technical fabrics, could save you several hundred dollars over the life of your hiking career. This edition also pays special attention to the ultralight materials that have become prevalent in outdoor gear in the last five years; they need special care, and Kristin shows you how.

Then, of course, there are Kristin's duct tape tricks, many of which I've used since she taught me to wrap a supply around my trekking poles many years ago. They're tried and true, and you shouldn't leave home without them.

Jonathan Dorn
Editor-in-Chief, *Backpacker*

ACKNOWLEDGMENTS

Being gear editor of *Backpacker* magazine certainly has its perks. Practically every day, the FedEx man delivers some shiny new product to my door—more tents, boots, packs, and bags than a person could ever need for a lifetime of adventures.

But when I took a four-year hiatus from my job to change diapers and feed and burp my two little boys, all that new gear stopped flowing in, and I had to resort to many of the repair and maintenance tips described in this book. During that time, I learned a lot of new techniques and honed some old ones, all of which are covered in this second edition.

Here's another thing I learned, after coming back to work after four years: Gear changes! In the short time I was gone, whole new categories grew from tiny, specialized niches to full-blown phenomena. Things like single-wall tents used to be the sole domain of alpinists and climbers; now just about every major tent manufacturer offers affordable single-walls that are light and breathable enough to appeal to the masses. Hydration systems—which were once the pet products of adventure racers and trail runners—are now a key feature in most backpacks, no matter what the size. Soft-shell fabrics were pretty much unheard-of back then; now they're all the rage in everything from pants and shorts to jackets and even hiking shoes. And technical wool, which had pretty much gone dormant in lieu of synthetic fabrics, has seen a huge rebirth in the base-layer and insulation categories.

Given all these changes, the time was ripe for a second edition.

I'd like to renew my thanks to all my colleagues at *Back-packer*—especially my friend and boss, Jon Dorn—who have taught me so many tricks over the years. I'd also like to thank George Farkus of McNett Corporation for taking so much time to educate me on adhesives and techniques. Thanks also to Bob Upton at Rainy Pass, who was always willing to lend advice.

Lastly, I'd like thank my two boys, Charlie and Joey, and Shaun, my husband. All working moms like to think that they can successfully juggle work and family. And though I try my hardest to know when to shut the office door and go out for a bike ride or kick around a soccer ball, there are times when I do the opposite. Thank you for putting up with me, and understanding that I love my work. But don't forget: I love you guys so much more.

INTRODUCTION

Glorious views. Peaceful gurgles of a brook. Happy chirpings of wild birds. Air so fresh that it cleanses to the core. The contented pride you get after a long day's hike. These are just some of the things we enjoy about camping and hiking.

But there is another, less obvious aspect of living in the wild that brings great satisfaction: complete independence from the civilized world. There's something deeply gratifying in knowing that you have the ability to carry everything you need to survive and prosper in a nylon sack strapped to your back. The happiest campers are the ones who strip away all the distractions and extraneous clutter of everyday life and make do with what's on hand. The first time you remedy a leak in your tent, fashion a new strap for your backpack, or nurse a cranky stove back to life, you experience a sort of epiphany: you are truly self-sufficient, a regular Grizzly Adams.

That is the philosophical, romantic reason for this book.

Of course, there are other, more practical ones. You'll save a bundle of money if you learn to maintain and fix damaged gear rather than replace it. You'll do the environment a great service if you keep your old gear working smoothly rather than banishing it to the landfills. And perhaps the most important reason of all: you'll enjoy your time spent in the wild if your equipment does not fail.

The goal of this book is to provide you with all the information and resources needed to care for and repair every item in your backpack—including the pack itself!

BACKPACKER'S REPAIR KIT

So what, you may ask, does it take to become an outdoor fix-it guru? Well, for starters, a good repair kit. Consider it your toolbox, a first-aid kit for your gear. A number of companies make and package basic gear-repair kits that are available at most outdoor shops.

You'll want to weed out some items and include some additional ones, based on your own gear and depending on the different types of trips you take. For instance, overnight and front-country trips don't require as deep a kit as a weeklong backcountry ramble. Some items you won't need to pack into the field, but you will want them at home for regular care and maintenance plus more elaborate repairs. The lists provided here are a good place to start.

Once your field repair kit is assembled, it will only weigh about half a pound. All the contents can be packed in a sturdy zippered pouch, stuff sack, or gallon-size, freezer-weight zipper-lock plastic bag.

When packing for your next backpacking trip, you might be tempted to jettison your repair kit along with your portable coffee-bean grinder and cushy camp chair. But don't! Hopefully you won't need a repair kit at all, but if your boot sole starts flapping and you don't have the goods to fix it, your whole trip will be ruined. Don't forget: a good repair kit is worth its weight in gorp.

Backpacking Repair-Kit Checklist
✓ good-quality duct tape
✓ assortment of fabric swatches (mosquito netting and light-weight ripstop nylon for tent, garment, and bag repairs)
✓ assortment of plastic buckles for pack repairs
✓ assortment of needles and safety pins (packed inside a 35mm film canister for safety)
✓ aluminum pole-repair sleeve
✓ adhesive/seam sealer such as Seam Grip

✓ 5–10 feet of nylon parachute cord
✓ dental floss
✓ thread
✓ a few heavy-duty rubber bands
✓ a lightweight multitool, preferably one that includes
  small pliers and scissors

At-Home Repair-Kit Checklist
✓ mild soap (not detergent) such as Ivory Flakes
✓ assortment of plastic-bristled brushes
✓ toothbrush
✓ irrigation syringe (for seam sealing)
✓ seam sealer
✓ boot goop (waterproofing agent and conditioner)
✓ assortment of waterproofing agents for tent, raingear, etc.
✓ pliers
✓ more duct tape (of course!)

DUCT TAPE TIP
Wrap a generous amount of duct tape around the middle
of a trekking pole, hiking staff, or flashlight, and leave the
bulky roll at home.

WHY DUCT TAPE RULES
Duct tape is the single most useful repair tool you can carry on
a backpacking trip, bar none. The best tape to use: standard-
grade (9mm), slick, silver fabric tape (not plastic). Opt for the
stickiest tape that pulls off the roll with the most resistance,
so it won't peel off if it becomes wet.

What else can fix pack, boots, tent, clothes, stove, filter, pad,
sunglasses, stuff sack, and your very own feet (see the next

section)? If you need convincing that duct tape is a worthwhile addition to your backpack, below are a few ingenious ways you might use it on your next hiking/camping trip.

NOTE: Many more duct tape ideas are scattered throughout the book—look for the Duct Tape Tip sidebars.

+ Got a gash on your rain jacket or backpack? Tape it up for a temporary fix.
+ Forgot your sunglasses leash? Your spoon? You can construct just about anything with a little imagination and a bit of duct tape.

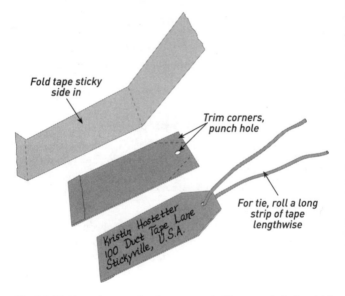

Fold tape sticky side in

Trim corners, punch hole

For tie, roll a long strip of tape lengthwise

Kristin Hostetter
100 Duct Tape Lane
Stickyville, U.S.A.

Fig. I-1. Making a luggage tag for your pack. These are indestructable and easy to spot on a conveyer belt.

+ Sore hips? If your pack's hip belt starts chafing during a trip, tape a tee shirt or some other piece of soft clothing to each pad of the hip belt.
+ Got binding blues? Skiers and snowshoers simply must carry a good supply of duct tape, which can be a lifesaver in the case of a blown binding or a bent or broken pole.
+ Close encounter with a cactus? Gently press a piece of duct tape to the spine-covered body part and pull the spines out in one fell swoop.
+ Boot laces keep untying? Lace them up, then tape them down.
+ Checking your pack on an airline? Make a duct-tape luggage tag that will last for years (fig. I-1).

Duct-Taping Blisters

Many people swear by duct tape for fixing foot woes, but unlike most other blister products, duct tape is not a cushy, comfy, tender-loving blister swaddler. Know how to use it properly so it does not exacerbate the damage.

+ Try taping over socks in problem areas or applying tape to pesky seams inside your boots.
+ Instead of applying sticky duct tape directly to a sore or blistered area, place a single layer of toilet paper over the skin, then apply the tape. Another solution is to use a second piece of duct tape, sticky side to sticky side, so that the smooth part is against the skin.
+ For additional stickiness, apply tincture of benzoin to the skin around the perimeter of your tape job.

 **FABRIC**

IMAGINE THIS:

The sun is finally shining after a few days of monsoonlike weather. You declare a rest day and spread all your gear out in the strong August sun to dry. Unfortunately, you unfurl your down sleeping bag a bit too close to a thorny blackberry bush, and now there's a two-inch gash spewing precious feathers over your campsite like snow. Are you doomed to watch as your cozy bag shrivels into a useless sack of nylon, or are you equipped with the supplies and skills for making a life-saving patch?

For the most part, the modern outdoorsperson uses gear and clothing made of lightweight synthetic fabrics or wool. Fleece, lightweight ripstop nylon, pack cloth, and heavier Cordura are some of the synthetic fabrics used for outdoor gear and clothing. Synthetics are ideal for outdoor use because they're rugged, they dry quickly, and they don't absorb water the way natural fibers such as cotton do. They're low-maintenance to boot.

Wool has made a big comeback in recent years. Clothes made from wool are tough, soft, and retain warmth when wet. Wool also tends to harbor less stink than synthetics, especially during sweaty activities. Wool requires a bit more caution when it comes to washing, but it is a great alternative, particularly in base layers, light insulation pieces, and socks.

Shelter from the elements is your number-one concern in the backcountry; arguably, the most sinister element you'll have to contend with is rain. Waterproof outdoor fabrics—like those that make up your outer-shell gear or tent—are either coated with a waterproofing potion or laminated to a waterproof/breathable membrane. The magic ingredient that makes water bead up and roll off all waterproof fabrics is called a DWR (durable, water-repellent) treatment.

QUALITY COUNTS

The thick, heavy, yellow-slicker material used for our childhood rain jackets really has no place in the wilds because the stuff, although perfectly waterproof, has zero breathability. If you tried hiking in a nonbreathable rain suit or sleeping in a nonbreathable tent, you would quickly be soaked not from the rain, but from your own perspiration and condensation buildup.

When buying any waterproof gear, look for factory-taped seams. You can see the outline of seam taping through the outside of the fabric (fig. 1-1a). If your raingear has any seams that are not taped (fig. 1-1b), apply a seam sealer, just as you would on a tent (see Chapter 5, Tents).

CARING FOR SYNTHETIC FABRICS

The most common problem with fleece is pilling. Over time, pilling is pretty much inevitable, but rest assured that it won't affect the performance of the fabric. If you want to groom your fleece jacket to make it look a bit fresher, brush the fabric with a pumice stone (the type used to remove calluses on feet works just fine) or a plastic-bristled kitchen brush.

Over time, the Velcro on all your gear will wind up caked with little fuzz balls that prevent it from doing its job. There

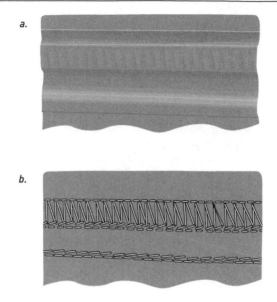

Fig. 1-1. Seams: a. taped seam, b. untaped seam

are two sides to Velcro: the hook (scratchy) side and the loop (fuzzy) side. Clean the hook side by scraping out debris with a fine-toothed comb. Put the loop side under the faucet and scrub it with an old toothbrush.

CLEANING SYNTHETIC FABRICS

Keep the fabrics of your gear clean, but resist the urge to wash them constantly. Do it on an as-needed basis to preserve their longevity. First rule: before laundering, always read the label. Synthetics can be washed in your home laundry machine using the gentle cycle, cold water, and mild soap. Your outdoor shop will carry some soaps made specifically for outdoor clothes. It may seem like an unnecessary investment when you have a gigantic bottle of laundry soap at home, but these specialized cleaners work very well and leave no residue on your gear.

AN OUNCE OF PREVENTION: BUTTON UP!

Before washing outdoor gear, make sure all zippers are zipped, snaps are snapped, and—this is important—Velcro is closed. This prevents the wear and tear of abrasion on the fabric.

The best way to wash your raingear is in front-loading commercial washers (found at a Laundromat) because they lack the spindle agitators that can be rough on your gear. Use cold water, the gentle cycle, and a mild laundry soap.

Because your synthetics will be virtually dry after undergoing the spin cycle of your washer, there's no need to throw them in the dryer. Just hang them up for a half hour or so, and they're ready for action. If you do want to put synthetics in your clothes dryer, again, read the label. As a general rule, synthetics can be dried in your dryer using the gentle/delicate setting and low/no heat.

CLEANING WOOL

For best results, turn your wool garments inside out before washing. Use cold water and a mild soap (like Woolite or Revivex Wool Cleaner, found at outdoor shops), and either hang dry or tumble dry on a low setting. (Most technical wool garments are pre-washed so shrinking won't be an issue. The exception is wool socks, which will sometimes tighten up a bit after laundering.) Some wool don'ts: steer clear of bleach, fabric softeners (they coat the fibers and inhibit breathability), and your friendly dry cleaner (unless the tag specifies it).

If you prefer to handwash your woolies, be sure to fill the tub or sink with enough cold water to submerge the garment, and one of the above soaps. Soak it for a few minutes, then gently knead the garment to release the dirt. After draining the sink, squeeze out any excess soap and water. Rinse continually until the water runs clear. Roll the item in a clean bath towel to soak up more water, then lay it out flat to dry.

REVIVING WATERPROOF FABRICS

You spend a bundle on your waterproof fabrics, but the time will come when your jacket or tent fly seems to be absorbing rain rather than repelling it. This is because the outer fabric's DWR treatment has worn off. Just like a good wax job on your car, this coating wears off over time, leaving you feeling wet even if no rain has actually penetrated the fabric.

When this happens, don't immediately go storming off to the shop that sold it to you. There are some simple, inexpensive things you can do to revive your waterproof gear if it starts to seep.

Wash it. Over time, dirt and things like campfire smoke get into the fabric and prevent the DWR treatment from doing its job. Some folks have gone years without washing their waterproof/breathable gear for fear that they will harm it. It may sound simple, but for the most part, occasional washing is a must. See Cleaning Synthetic Fabrics earlier in this chapter.

Machine-dry it. Machine-drying on a medium setting will reactivate the DWR coating that's left in the fabric, unless the manufacturer recommends otherwise. (See Cleaning Synthetic Fabrics.)

COMPARING DWR TREATMENTS

	Pros	Cons
Spray-on treatments	Tend to repel rain a bit better.	Tough to get a perfectly smooth, even coating.
Wash-in treatments	Easy and clean to apply, and you get a perfectly distributed coating.	Wicking inner liners get coated too and perform-ance can suffer.

Table 1-1.

Iron it. As strange as it may sound, carefully running a warm iron (on a low setting) over your waterproof garment brings even more of those DWR molecules to life. Before ironing, be sure to wipe down the iron to make sure it's clean.

Check the seams. If your seam tape is peeling or leaking, send it back to the manufacturer for repair. It's always under warranty.

Reapply a DWR treatment. If you do all of the above steps and rain still doesn't bead up and run off your garment, it means your existing DWR treatment is all but gone and it is time to apply a new one. There are a number of good DWR treatments on the market, available as either spray-on or wash-in; Table 1-1 lists the advantages and disadvantages of each.

For a **spray-on** treatment, hang the garment outdoors or in a well-ventilated place. Use long, uniform strokes and try to prevent drips. It's better to apply two light coats rather than one thick one. Give extra attention (a few extra layers) to abrasion-prone areas like shoulders, cuffs, and hip-belt areas.

For a **wash-in** treatment, pre-wash the garment. Fill the drum of the washing machine with water, add the treatment, wait a few minutes, then add the garment and complete the wash cycle, but *stop before it hits rinse*, or all that treatment will be flushed away. Then pop it into the dryer for a few minutes to set the treatment.

TIP: Fleece garments can also be treated with wash-in solutions. Of course, a fleece jacket will never be fully waterproof, but it will repel rain much better with a little help.

REPAIRING SYNTHETIC FABRICS

Learn these techniques and you'll be ready to repair just about anything, from a small hole in your clothing or backpack to a gaping slash in your tent or sleeping bag.

Fixing Small Gashes

For small wounds in your hard- or soft-shell raingear, pack, or tent, there's no need to bust out the needle and thread. Duct tape works in a pinch, but when removed, duct tape leaves a sticky residue that is almost impossible to repair. There are a couple of easy no-sew repair options:

A self-sticking patch. A number of companies offer this type of product, either in pre-cut patches or in tape-like rolls. Tenacious Tape by McNett is one of the best. Simply clean the area with an alcohol prep pad from your first-aid kit, then join the edges as best as possible on a flat surface. Smooth the patching material (always be sure to cut the patch so that it has rounded edges) over the gash, using pressure from the center outward to remove air bubbles. Then, for added strength, apply an identical patch to the other side of the fabric.

A urethane plug. This technique works well for pinprick holes and small, clean tears. You'll need a tube of the ubiquitous Seam Grip. Place a piece of paper or duct tape on the backside of the problem spot. Spread Seam Grip over the hole with about a ¼-inch overhang and let it cure 8–10 hours. Remove the tape.

The Perfect Patch

If sewing is in order (because of a large or jagged rip or your lack of other, easier-to-use materials), fear not. You don't need to be Martha Stewart in order to fix torn outdoor gear. All you need is a sturdy needle, the right sort of thread, and a swatch of fabric—preferably one similar in weight to the one you are repairing—big enough to cover the damaged area. Here is a step-by-step guide to patching just about anything:

1. Using scissors, cut a rounded patch of fabric bigger than the hole or damaged area by about one inch on all sides.

2. Turn the item inside out and lay the patch in place. Avoid pinning it in place because this can cause more damage to the fabric—especially if it's waterproof.

3. Make small, tightly spaced overhand stitches (see Stitches

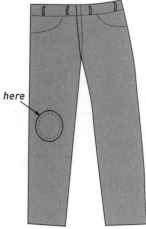

Seal here

Fig. 1-2. Patching

You Should Know, below) around the patch and tie it off securely on the back.

4. Seam-seal around the stitch lines if necessary (fig. 1-2).

Stitches You Should Know

Overhand stitch. This is perfect for patching holes in sleeping bag shells, clothing, or tent walls. Simply loop the needle through the fabric layers so that the stitches make little parallel slanting lines (fig. 1-3a). This is the simplest of stitches—even if you have ten thumbs.

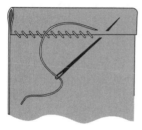
a.

b.

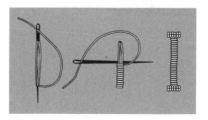
c.

Fig. 1-3. Basic stitches: a. overhand, b. backstitch, c. bar tack

Backstitch. This is ideal for repairing seam tears or patching when strength is more an issue. You reinforce each stitch by doubling back over it (fig. 1-3b).

Bar tack. This is great for fixing blown pack straps or mending pocket tears. Make three to five long stitches running parallel to the tear. Then make a zillion small, tight overhand stitches across the long ones to close the gap. Augment the repair with tiny bar stitches at either end, so that the finished work resembles a capital "I" (fig. 1-3c).

REPAIRING MOSQUITO NETTING
There is nothing more annoying than an elusive mosquito making kamikaze runs at your ears all night long. That's why it pays to know what to do if the mosquito netting on your tent, garment, or hat gets a gash.

Large tears or holes can be patched using the swatch of mosquito netting from your repair kit and a simple overhand stitch (see Stitches You Should Know, above). If the hole is smaller than one inch in diameter, try this handy technique:

1. Place a piece of paper (the table of contents from your

DUCT TAPE TIP
Resist the urge to make a quick duct-tape patch on fabric unless you absolutely have to. The tape will eventually peel away and leave a sticky residue on the fabric, which makes permanent repairs more difficult. Instead, use one of the techniques for repairing synthetic fabrics listed in this section, or retire to your tent a little early and practice your sewing skills. In the long run, you'll be much happier—and so will your gear.

novel will do just fine) over the hole (either side of the fabric is fine) and secure it with duct tape.

2. Turn the fabric over and smear a generous amount of Seam Grip over the paper-backed hole, smoothing it into a sheet.

3. After the Seam Grip has cured completely (ideally, 48 hours), peel off the tape and paper, leaving the Seam Grip filling the hole. **NOTE:** Do not pack the tent, garment, or hat until the Seam Grip is totally dry—you could create a massive knot of fabric and glue that would be nearly impossible to fix in the field.

 **ZIPPERS**

IMAGINE THIS:
You're 20 miles from the nearest trailhead when your pack explodes all over the pine needles. Spontaneous combustion? Not quite. The U-shaped zipper on your pack's front panel finally succumbed to the stresses of overload and physical abuse. Will a whole lot of luck and duct tape put your pack back together again? Or do you know how to handle a zipper emergency?

Zippers adorn nearly every piece of soft gear that accompanies you into the wilds—clothes, tent, bag, pack. There are two basic kinds of zippers: coiled and toothed.

Most of the zippers you'll find on outdoor gear are coil zippers, made from tiny loops or coils sewn into the zipper tape fabric. The beauty of coil zips is that they are often self-healing, meaning that when a crimp in one of the coils happens, all you do is pass the slider (the tab you grab and slide up and down) back and forth, and the coils straighten themselves out.

Toothed zippers—with their interlocking wedge-shaped

QUALITY COUNTS

When it comes to zippers, beefier is better. Also, opt for coil zippers over toothed zippers. Coils are much easier to repair.

teeth—are generally less desirable than coil zips because once a tooth breaks, there is nothing you can do short of replacing the whole zipper.

The ubiquitous zipper is a wonderful invention. The problem is, zippers tend to break—so it pays to know how to fix them. If you don't know what to do, a zapped zipper can be a major disaster, especially if the nighttime temperature has dropped like an anchor and your tent door is flapping in the breeze. This chapter teaches you how to fix the four most common zipper failures—crushed coils, broken teeth, a worn slider, and a broken pull—and to care for your zippers so these things never happen in the first place.

AN OUNCE OF PREVENTION: DON'T YANK!

Pulling on a zipper to unstick it only mangles the slider and causes more problems. Treat your zippers kindly, and they will continue to work for you indefinitely.

CLEANING ZIPPERS

If your zippers seem balky, it may be because grit is living inside the teeth or coils. Using a damp toothbrush, scrub the zipper on both sides, then let it air dry. Avoid lubricating it with oil or silicone spray, as this just attracts more dirt.

REPAIRING CRUSHED OR DAMAGED COILS

Sometimes those coils get crushed beyond the point of self-healing. If this happens, try to reshape the coils by inserting a sewing needle or straightened safety pin underneath one coil at a time and gently pulling the coil upward and back into shape (fig. 2-1). If the coils look rough or full of burrs, try gently filing them smooth with an emery board.

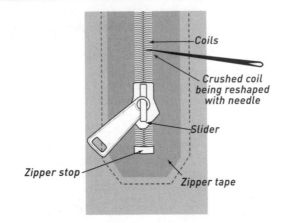

Fig. 2-1. Coil zipper

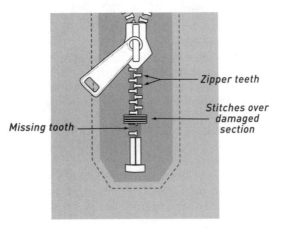

Fig. 2-2. Toothed zipper

REPAIRING A BROKEN ZIPPER TOOTH

If you're in the field and need that broken zipper to function till the end of your trip, get out your needle and thread and sew the zipper shut where the tooth is missing (fig. 2-2). At the very least, your zipper will work up to that point, and you can replace it with a proper coil zipper when you get back home.

REPAIRING A WORN SLIDER

You're strolling down the trail when a chilly gust of wind reminds you to zip up your jacket. When you do, the zipper inexplicably pops open in the middle. This is the symptom of the most common zipper ailment: a worn slider. When a slider gets worn, its shape changes slightly so it can't properly align the two sides of the zipper.

How does a slider wear out? Regular, proper use usually is not enough to damage a good slider. But if dirt or grit finds its way inside or along the coils themselves, the damage can be quick and lethal. Even more common is general abuse. How many times have you gotten frustrated with your zipper, then yanked and yanked and yanked on it until it finally surrendered? Or when a bit of fabric gets jammed, do you jerk on the

AN OUNCE OF PREVENTION: ATTENTION ULTRALIGHTERS!

The ultralight craze has reached epidemic proportions. Modern-day gear weighs a fraction of what it used to, and zippers are no exception. Be very gentle with those featherweight zippers on your new four-ounce rain jacket. They're even more susceptible to malfunction. Be sure to properly align the zipper sides before pulling on the slider, and stop yanking if you encounter a snag.

zipper and try to strong-arm it into submission? Well, that's the sort of thing that hurts zippers most.

The good news is that many sliders can be repaired using only a small set of pliers—the type found on many pocket tools. In the case of the fabric getting caught in the zipper, use your pliers to gently pull the fabric out. In the case of a worn, tired, or misshapen slider, open the zipper all the way up. Next, use your pliers to very gently pinch one of the two openings a little more closed (fig. 2-3). Then pinch the other side, using equal pressure. Try the zipper. Repeat this gradual pinching process until the slider is sufficiently tightened and your zipper stays zipped.

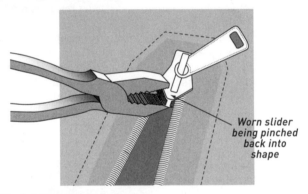

Worn slider being pinched back into shape

Fig. 2-3. Repairing a worn slider

REPAIRING A BROKEN, LOST, OR INADEQUATE ZIPPER PULL

It happens all the time. The little grab-tab on the end of the zipper either disappears or is simply so small that you need a set of tweezers to find it. If this happens, simply remove the old tab and attach a new and improved one. You are limited only by your imagination. Use ribbon, cord, a paper clip, a whistle, or a thermometer. Generally speaking, the bigger the pull the better, especially if it is a zipper you intend to use while wearing gloves or mittens.

DUCT TAPE TIP
Make a sturdy zipper pull by threading a thin strip of duct tape through the slider, then wrapping the tails with more duct-tape strips (fig 2-4).

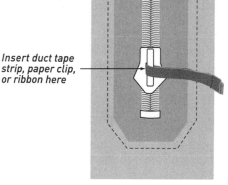

Insert duct tape strip, paper clip, or ribbon here

Fig. 2-4. Duct tape puller

 **BOOTS**

IMAGINE THIS:
You spent all day slogging across streams and through puddles, and now your boots are sodden, cold, leather foot-prisons. You snuggle up to a crackling fire, doff your boots, and place them near the heat to dry out. The next morning your boots are cozy and dry, but also a full size smaller! After a mile on the trail, the heat-shrunken leather has chafed your heels into oozing craters of flesh. Could you have spared yourself this agony and still walked away with dry feet?

A good pair of boots should last for many years, provided that you care for them properly. Most boot problems happen over time, so regular inspection of and prompt attention to the soles, seams, and materials can save you from a major blowout.

QUALITY COUNTS
If you often find yourself in wet conditions, invest in boots with a waterproof/breathable liner, like Gore-Tex or eVent (up to $50 more). They may make your feet sweat a bit more, and you still have to treat the leather portions, but unless water spills over the boot tops, you will not get soaked in waterproof/breathable boots. Period.

BREAKING IN NEW BOOTS
When you invest in a new pair of boots, you immediately want to take them on a hike, just like when you get a new car and

can't wait for that first drive. But resist that temptation and give yourself ample time to break in new boots. The heavier and stiffer the boots, the more break-in time they'll need, but even the lightest-weight hiking boots deserve a few days of test runs before they hit the trail just to be sure the fit is perfect.

The best tool for breaking in new boots is one we never seem to have: time. The moment you get home from the store, put your new boots on and wear them around the house for a few days. This will give you time to be sure you've made the right decision without gunking up the boots so badly that the store will not take them back. (Most good stores will let you return the boots after a few days, as long as they're still clean and have not been worn outside.)

Once you're satisfied that you've made the right choice, start wearing your boots on errands around town—walking the dog, to the market, etc. Wear them to the office if you can—the more wear time, the better. After a few days, it's safe to start taking them on day hikes. Then you can gradually build up to longer trips.

Sometimes, though, we don't have the luxury of time, so below are a few tips that will help you speed up the process. These tips are geared mostly toward unruly leather boots. For lightweight fabric–leather boots, you shouldn't have to resort to any of these methods.

The Full Wetting

This works best for all-leather (including the lining) boots. Wear the boots down to your favorite creek. Walk into the creek until water pours over the top and into your boots. Stand there until the boots are thoroughly soaked—inside and out. If it is chilly, you may want to wear Gore-Tex socks over your hiking socks to keep your feet dry. Then go for a long hike and wear the boots until they dry. Once dry, they will have magically molded to your feet and all their quirky contours. After their dunk, be sure to treat them with a moisturizing boot goop (see Waterproofing Leather Boots, below).

Leather Softeners
A thin application of Lexol or any other oil-based leather treatment softens the leather so that it can more easily mold to your feet. On lighter-weight boots, though, beware: Oversoftening can lead to boots that have little or no support.

Rubbing Bar
If there's a specific area that keeps bothering you, such as near your piggy toe or at the base of your big toe, try this method. First, soften the area on the boot with a bit of Lexol or mink oil. Then, using a smooth, blunt, hard object, like the end of your (closed) pocketknife or the end of a broomstick, repeatedly rub the offending area into submission. In essence, you're creating a pocket of space for that part of your foot.

WATERPROOFING LEATHER BOOTS
Few things in outdoor life are more depressing than cold, wet, pruney feet. By applying a waterproofer properly and in a timely manner, you not only help to keep your feet dry and warm, you're also feeding and nurturing the leather, which extends its life span and performance.

The key to maintaining the health of your boots' leather is to try to keep it at an equilibrium. Overly wet leather is prone to tearing; overly dry leather is prone to cracking. By applying the right stuff at the right time, you keep the leather supple, healthy, and strong.

What is the right stuff? There are loads of good waterproofers out there, all tailored to work with different types of leather and materials. Talk to a knowledgeable salesperson about what type will work best with the boots you have. Avoid using mink oil, which will oversoften most backpacking and hiking boots. **NOTE:** If your intent is to simply soften stiff, unyielding leather, a dab of mink oil may help.

Whichever treatment you use, be sure to follow the instructions carefully. Two or three thin coats are better than one thick, gloppy one. Also, contrary to some old-timers' opinions, you should never warm your boots in the oven prior to treatment—unless you want the toes to curl up like clown shoes and the glue to melt all over the place.

When is the right time to treat your boots? Depending on the amount of wear they get, boots will need treating about one to three times a year, or whenever the leather starts to lighten in color and look dry and thirsty.

A few more treatment tips:

✦ Before you start working, take out the laces and pull out the tongue. First, clean your boots. Using a sponge and water or a boot cleaner (you'll find a selection at your outdoor shop), remove any dirt or grime. Let the boots dry completely. **TIP:** Stuffing them with newspaper will speed things along.

✦ Apply your chosen boot goop in a thin, even coat. Don't forget all the little nooks and crannies—such as in the tongue gussets and around each eyelet.

✦ After the boot goop has had ample curing time, buff the boots with a boot brush. This is not to make them look nattier, though they surely will, but to smooth and harden the finish. If after a day or so your boots still feel tacky or there is a visible waxy buildup, you may have been overly generous with your goop. Wipe off the excess with a rag, and buff until they are smooth.

+ For fabric-leather boots with multiple seams, seal the seams with an irrigation syringe before you waterproof the boots. Purchase a can of spray-on fabric waterproofing treatment for the fabric portions of the boots. The leather can be treated as discussed above, but the fabric requires a different sort of concoction.

CARING FOR YOUR BOOTS

When you reach the car after a wet, mucky hike, don't stuff your poor, hardworking boots into a plastic bag and then toss them into a corner of the basement. A week later, when you open that bag, you'll find a science project—colonies of mold and mildew in the shape of a boot.

AN OUNCE OF PREVENTION: DRY SLOWLY

Never dry wet boots near a fire or other heat source, unless you want to destroy them, shrink them, or both. The best way to dry boots is slowly but surely. Remove the insoles and laces. Open the boots up as much as possible for maximum airflow. Insert newspaper. If you're in the field, try chemical heating packs/handwarmers.

Find yourself a good local cobbler who has experience with hiking boots to assist you with major repairs. Especially if your boots are expensive, leave big jobs to the pros. That said, there are some things you should know about dealing with problems that occur while you're out on the trail.

REPAIRING PEELING SOLES

If your boots are old-school Norwegian-welted boots (they have a visible line of stitching where sole meets leather), don't try to repair any of the stitching yourself—trust it to a cobbler. However, most boots these days have soles that are glued, rather than stitched, to the upper, and with a bit of effort, you can probably do a pretty good repair job on your own.

If your boot sole starts flapping in the field, your only real choice is to duct-tape it thoroughly and hope it holds till you make it home. Once you and the boot are home, here's an easy six-step procedure to fix the problem.

1. Start by making sure the boot is clean. Wash it with soap and water and let it dry completely before proceeding. Then wipe down the area in question with alcohol and let it air dry completely. Repeat this alcohol wash two or three times to be sure all the oils and waxes are removed.

2. Cram the boot toe with socks or newspaper. This ensures that the boot retains its proper shape under the pressure you are about to exert.

3. Using a good contact cement designed for shoe repair (Freesole, Shoe Goo, and Barge are three examples), smear the leather and the sole where the two were once joined— and will be again! Wait until the cement is almost dry but still tacky.

4. Next, carefully press the sole into place on the upper. Use a steady hand, and be sure to mate the two pieces accurately; once they touch, the cemented parts are just that— cemented.

5. Place a full water bottle or a bunch of rocks into the boot to weight it down and hold the sole in place. Let the boot rest until the cement is totally, completely, thoroughly, 100 percent dry (this may take up to 48 hours for thick applications).

6. Last, inject seam sealer into the joint with an irrigation syringe.

DUCT TAPE TIP

When regluing a boot sole, a few turns of duct tape can keep the toe area secure while the glue dries (fig. 3-1).

Fig. 3-1. Fixing a peeling boot sole. A few turns of duct tape are ideal for keeping the toe area secure while curing.

REPAIRING PEELING TOE RANDS

The toe rand is the protective bumper of rubber that surrounds the toe area of many boots. Since this area takes a lot of abuse on the trail, the rand can sometimes begin to peel away from the boot. But that's no reason to go shopping for new boots. The fix is easy—a variation on Repairing Peeling Soles, above.

1. First, lightly sand the toe area and buff it with alcohol. Let it dry completely, then wipe with alcohol again.
2. Stuff the boot tightly with socks or newspaper to retain its shape.
3. Squeeze some urethane cement (such as Freesole) into the gap between the peeling rand and the leather, and rejoin the two pieces.

4. Place a ballpoint pen against the repaired section of the rubber rand (this applies direct pressure to the repair), and securely wrap with duct tape. Allow it to cure for up to 48 hours, then remove the tape (fig. 3-2).

ballpoint pen

toe rand

Fig. 3-2. Repairing a peeling toe rand. Use a ballpoint pen to concentrate the pressure.

FIXING SMALL TEARS AND HOLES

Small gashes and tiny puncture holes in leather can be remedied by using a bit of adhesive. Seam Grip will work in a pinch, but boots are best patched using a urethane specifically designed for the task, such as Freesole. Just smooth a clump of the sticky stuff into the cleaned and prepped wound, then let it rest until thoroughly cured. Larger openings will require the services of a cobbler.

REBUILDING WORN HEELS

Walk enough miles in any boot and the heel will start to show signs of wear. But if the rest of the boot is still in solid shape, there's a way to rebuild your worn heel and get some more miles out of it.

1. Start by sanding the worn area lightly, then rub with an alcohol-soaked rag to remove any grimy residue.
2. Make a duct-tape dam by wrapping a piece of duct tape around the heel of the boot, leaving about an inch of overhang (fig. 3-3).
3. Prop the boot heel-side up, so that the heel area is level. Spread a thick layer of Freesole over the worn area, smoothing it to the same level as the undamaged portion of the sole.
4. Let cure for a solid 24 hours.

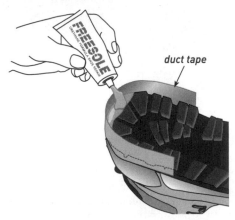

duct tape

Fig. 3-3. Rebuilding worn heels. Make a dam of duct tape, and then apply Freesole to the worn area.

MAKING A TOE CAP ON LEATHER BOOTS

The top of the boot toe area withstands untold abuse, and is often the first part of the leather to show signs of fatigue. If your boot toes are starting to look bashed, this is a quick and easy remedy that will protect them for many more miles.

1. As always, clean the area in question and let it dry thoroughly. Apply a length of duct tape in a straight line

Fig. 3-4. Making a toe cap. Use duct tape to create a straight edge, and then paint a protective layer of Freesole over the toe.

across the part of the boot where the base of your toes would be (fig. 3-4a).

2. Lightly sand the toe area, then rub aggressively with an alcohol-soaked rag. Let it dry, then rub it a second time with alcohol.

3. Using a small brush, paint the toe area thoroughly with a thin layer of Freesole, right up to the duct tape, which creates a straight edge (fig. 3-4b).

4. After about 45 minutes, remove the tape and let your new toe caps cure for at least 12 hours (fig. 3-4c).

 **PACKS**

IMAGINE THIS:
After an extravagant lunch of salami and Swiss cheese bagels, you dread donning your gigantic pack for the five-mile march to tonight's camp. You take a deep breath, grab a shoulder strap, and brace yourself for your sadistic load. Pop! The webbing explodes from the pack bag, leaving you with a dangling strap and a small gaping hole, neither of which will do, considering there is no wheelbarrow handy to ferry your busted pack down the trail. Do you sit down on a rock and wait for the search and rescue crew? Or do you have what it takes to fix the fix you are in?

Backpacks come in three basic constructions: external-frame, internal-frame, and frameless rucksack. External-frame packs are kind of like Volkswagen Beetles: they were all the rage back in the 60s and 70s, then they pretty much died out of fashion. The majority of large packs that are sold today are internals, which hug your body and move with you, making them ideal for climbing, bushwhacking, and rugged off-trail travel. Still, many hikers who stick to long, hot, and well-trod trails may find that external-frame packs carry the load more comfortably and allow for better ventilation. Frameless rucksacks are the most common type of day pack, as the lack of a structural support system makes them suitable only for light loads.

CARING FOR YOUR PACK
Here are some tips to ensure your pack a longer life:
At home, inspect the inside seams of the pack. If any fabric

QUALITY COUNTS

Because your pack will often be filled to the gills with heavy gear, its seams need to be burly enough to handle the pressure. Check the pack's innards for tight, finished seams, and beware of loose, fraying ends or single stitching. And although supercushy foam in the pack's waist belt and shoulder straps may sound like a good idea and feel good at first, it often turns into a pancake after a bit of use. Look for foam that's soft yet dense, so that it will not won't lose its integrity over the long haul.

edges are fraying, trim them neatly with scissors so they don't snag in the pack's zippers. Better yet, smear the fraying edge with Seam Grip for permanent prevention.

When packing your pack, make sure sharp objects such as tent stakes, tent poles, and stoves are padded so they don't rub against the inside of your pack and cause a rip.

At rest breaks on the trail, instead of dropping your pack down with a thump, remember how much it cost, then set it down gently instead.

AN OUNCE OF PREVENTION: PACK COVERS

Because of their multiple, complicated seams and rugged, porous fabrics, backpacks by themselves are rarely totally waterproof. To keep your backpack and all its contents dry, invest in a nylon pack cover or siliconized-nylon pack liner. If your pack cover's waterproofing starts to get tired, it can be recoated just like a tent fly (see Chapter 5, Tents).

Keep your pack food-free. Make sure to remove any food crumbs from the pockets and recesses of your pack, both in the field and for long-term storage at home. Little woodland critters think nothing of chewing a hole through nylon, even for a tiny cookie crumb.

CLEANING YOUR PACK

Granola crumbs, bug repellent, and plain old sweat are some of the things that can turn your pack into a grimy, stinky sack. You will probably need to wash your pack only every couple of seasons or so—unless a calamity such as a leaky fuel bottle happens (see An Ounce of Prevention: Double-Bag Liquids).

Fill a bucket with warm water and a bit of dissolved soap (Ivory Flakes or a mild dishwashing soap will do). Using a vegetable brush, scrub every inch of the pack, inside and out, including all the corners, sweaty straps, zippers, and buckles. Give the whole pack a good, high-pressure rinse with a garden hose and hang it outside to air dry.

AN OUNCE OF PREVENTION: DOUBLE-BAG LIQUIDS

A leaky bottle of liquid—cooking oil, sticky beverages, sunscreen, or the like—can be a debacle, not only for all the gear in your pack but for the pack itself. Double-bag bottles of liquids inside freezer-weight zipper-lock bags, then pack them far away from your food and clothes, preferably in their own side pocket.

REPAIRING EXTERNAL PACK FRAMES

Pack disasters that don't involve zippers or fabrics are rare, but occasionally you'll need to make field repairs on the pack's frame. The good thing about external aluminum frames is that they most often bend before they break, giving you the opportunity to make the repair before a total blowout occurs. If an aluminum frame bends, try to gently bend it back, and make a precautionary splint so it doesn't break the next time you drop your pack.

In case the frame on an external-frame pack does break, all you need to do is fashion a makeshift splint. Your options for materials are limited only by your imagination: a tent stake, a cut-up aluminum can wrapped around the frame, or a sturdy stick will do the trick when secured around the bend or break with a healthy dose of duct tape.

REPAIRING PACK BUCKLES

For starters, always make sure your repair kit includes spare buckles that match the critical ones on your pack. Buckle breaks are rare, but if they do occur—especially the large hip belt buckle—and you don't have the means to fix it, your shoulders will hate you for making them bear the brunt of your load.

The second critical pack buckle that could break is located on your pack straps—the tension buckles that allow you to cinch the shoulder straps tight and shift the weight around. If one of these breaks, you will have to cut the webbing, then

Slot

Fig. 4-1. Spare tension buckle. This type is ideal for repairs because of the slot. No need for sewing.

sew it shut around a new buckle, unless you happen to have a spare that is designed for such purposes (fig. 4-1). These handy repair buckles have a slot on the second bar that allows you to simply slip the webbing loop right back into place.

REPAIRING PACK STRAPS

If the scenario described at the beginning of this chapter happens to you, no amount of duct tape will save you. Luckily, a dip into your well-stocked sewing kit and about 20 minutes of careful stitching are all that stand between you and happy trails. Chances are, the strap blowout happened where the webbing strap attaches to the nylon of the pack bag, sandwiched inside a side seam.

Turn the pack bag inside out and, from the outside, poke the orphaned strap back through the original opening. Using your largest needle and a strong polyester thread, fashion a sturdy bar tack (see Stitches You Should Know in Chapter 1, Fabric) that reattaches the webbing to the two layers of fabric (fig. 4-2).

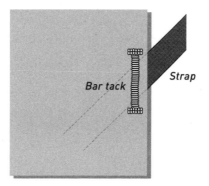

Fig.4-2. Fixing a strap blowout

FIXING A GASH

Large tears in pack fabric can be sewn and seam-sealed, while smaller rips and holes can be fixed easily and permanently using the urethane-plug technique described in Chapter 1 under Repairing Synthetic Fabrics, Fixing Small Gashes.

DUCT TAPE TIP

If the female (socket) side of your pack's hip-belt buckle cracks or breaks and you find yourself without a spare, you can hold it together with a few wraps of duct tape until you get back home.

 **5** **TENTS**

IMAGINE THIS:
You are three days into a weeklong hike through a remote wilderness. While stopping for a rest break under gathering storm clouds, you gratefully ditch your overloaded pack. It lands with a thud and a loud snap. Upon inspection, you discover that one of the four tent poles strapped to the outside of your pack has snapped. Have you packed the necessary tools to repair the pole and guarantee a dry, comfortable night? Or will you be soggy and cold in a droopy tent?

This chapter covers all types and shapes of double-wall and single-wall tents. For extensive repairs, you may want to consider calling in the experts (see the appendix, Repair Facility Reference Guide, at the back of this book).

QUALITY COUNTS

When shopping for a new tent, be sure to set it up and stake it out tightly (most stores provide Velcro "carpet stakes") to be sure the tent is taut and tightly sewn together. You should be able to bounce a quarter off any given side of a well-made tent. This means the tent will send precipitation bouncing away from you when bad weather strikes.

PACKING YOUR TENT

There are two schools of thought on tent packing. "Rollers" meticulously lay out the tent, fold it neatly into thirds, then roll it up like a sleeping pad, and slip it into its sack. If you are the rolling type, just be sure to shift the fold line every now and then to avoid permanently creasing the fabric and possibly cracking any waterproof coating.

"Crammers" simply open the mouth of the stuff sack and start stuffing—first the fly, then the tent body, or vice versa. This method may go against your fervent desire to pamper your sizable investment, but most seasoned outdoorsfolk opt for cramming. It's so much faster and easier, especially if the stuff sack is on the smallish side.

AN OUNCE OF PREVENTION: BAG YOUR STAKES

Be sure to pack tent stakes in their own small but rugged sack so there is no chance they will puncture or tear the delicate tent fabric in transit.

PREVENTING CONDENSATION

Oftentimes it's not an actual tent leak that gets you wet, but condensation buildup inside the tent—the result of your and your tentmates' breathing all night. Some tents have well-placed windows and vents, and therefore are inherently better at battling condensation, but a few techniques will help you win the war in any tent.

Setup

First, be sure to set up your tent properly. This may seem obvious, but many people just shove the poles in their sleeves and call it good. For a supertaut pitch that will have water pinging off your rain fly, start by staking out each and every spot on your tent's floor to give you maximum interior space.

Then attach the fly and repeat the process, using all the available stake-out loops and guy lines. Install line tensioners, little aluminum or plastic figure-eight-like gadgets, on all your guy lines. These allow you to easily stake out a guy line, then tighten it without moving the stake (especially helpful on rocky ground where it is tough to find a secure position for stakes).

Placement

Try to pitch your tent on high ground, where you're more likely to catch a little breeze. If the wind is really howling, pitch the lowest side of the tent (often the foot end) into the wind to create a more aerodynamic shape. If the weather is still and steamy, pitch the biggest expanse of mesh (often the door) facing the wind.

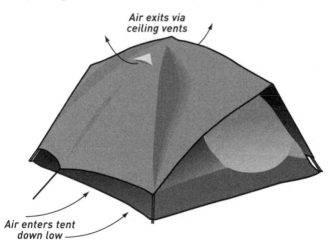

Fig. 5-1. High-low venting, a.k.a. the chimney effect

Airflow

Once your tent is erected, use the windows and door(s) to achieve optimum airflow inside. Ideally, you want to create the chimney effect, where cool air comes into your tent from down low and has a place to exit up high (fig. 5-1). Play around with the zippers on the windows and door(s) to get the best high/low airflow.

CLEANING AND STORING YOUR TENT

A tent's number-one enemy is unchecked moisture. Tents can remain erect in the rain indefinitely with no damage, but if you pack a sodden tent into its stuff sack and leave it there for a day or two, it's doomed. It will become infested with mold and mildew that can weaken the waterproof coating and the fabric itself, plus leave your backwoods abode with a perpetual stink. The moral: Be sure to unpack a wet tent as soon as possible and set it up to dry, preferably in a sunny, breezy place.

Eventually your tent will succumb to the griminess of outdoor living. Dead mosquitoes smeared against the interior walls, dried mud and spilled food on the floor, sand stuck in the zippers—these are all par for the course in the wilderness. At some point you'll have to resort to soap and water.

You may be thinking...hey, it is made of fabric just like my raingear, so why not toss it in the washing machine and be done in a snap? Because tents—with their mosquito netting and special waterproof coatings—are too delicate for the likes of your washing machine. It doesn't take long to do the job right, and hand-washing gives you the chance to closely inspect every square inch of the tent for wear, tear, and downright damage.

Erect your tent on a grassy patch of yard. Dissolve a mild soap (such as Ivory Flakes) into a big bucket of water and start scrubbing with a large car-wash-style sponge. Use a fingernail or vegetable brush on the webbing stake-out loops and zipper tracks. Finish with a good blast from the garden hose, then let your tent air dry completely.

Removing Mildew Stench

If you've already washed your tent as described above and the stench of mildew won't quit, try this two-step process:

1. Combine ½ cup of Lysol and one gallon of hot water. Use a big sponge to wash the tent thoroughly with this concoction, then let it air dry.

2. Combine one cup of salt, one cup of concentrated lemon juice, and one gallon of hot water. Give your tent a sponge bath with this solution, then let it air dry. **NOTE:** This technique will remove the smell of mildew, but not the stain.

Another option: Try McNett's Mirazyme, a microbe- and enzyme-based solution that works well. Fill the bathtub with enough water to cover the tent and add Mirazyme per the instructions on the bottle. Open all the zippers and plop the tent into the solution, making sure all the fabric goes under. Soak

AN OUNCE OF PREVENTION: UV DAMAGE

It may sound like fun to leave your tent set up in the backyard for the kids to play in, but don't. Aside from killing the patch of grass underneath it, you'd be subjecting your tent to unneccessary UV rays, which can weaken the fabric and coatings over time. Normal use will not inflict UV damage to your tent, so don't worry about using it on a sunny, weeklong trip. But whenever possible choose a site that is at least partially shaded, and don't leave the tent set up in the sun any longer than necessary.

for about 10 minutes, then hang the tent on a line in the shade. When the tent is thoroughly dry, the stench should be gone.

POLES

Tent poles are the skeleton of your shelter. Just as you would be unable to function without your bones, your tent is hard-pressed to do its job of protecting you without its poles. With their bendy shapes that are perfectly sized for your particular tent, poles are almost impossible to improvise but are very easy to fix, provided you have the right stuff.

QUALITY COUNTS

Aluminum tent poles perform better than fiberglass ones, which are prone to splintering and snapping. Of course, aluminum poles add to the tent's price, but the expense is well worth it in the long run. Some ultralight tents come equipped with carbon fiber poles, which shave weight but require extra care (they're more fragile than aluminum).

Cleaning Tent Poles

It's a good idea to keep your pole joints clean and grit-free. If you hear or feel some scratching when you're fitting the poles together, simply dunk the joints into water and dry them thoroughly.

Straightening a Bent Pole

The most common cause of bent poles: the combination of extremely high winds and not guying out the tent sufficiently. With a bit of finesse, most aluminum poles can be reshaped. Place the bent section over your knee, grasping the ends of the section with your hands. Very gently, and just a little at a time, pull on the ends until you feel the pole start to yield. Check your progress frequently, and keep reshaping until the pole is back to normal. If you're too aggressive with your efforts and a kink or crease happens, read the next section.

Repairing a Broken Pole

If you don't have the right tools, a broken pole can be a tragedy that renders your otherwise hardy shelter a droopy, flapping mess of nylon. Good thing the remedy is featherweight and foolproof: a small aluminum repair sleeve that probably came standard with the purchase of your tent.

Simply slide the tube over the broken section and duct tape it securely into place (fig. 5-2). Take care when sliding this section into and out of the pole sleeve, because it will tend to snag on the fabric.

Back at home, contact the tent manufacturer about fixing or replacing the injured pole; most are covered under an unlimited warranty.

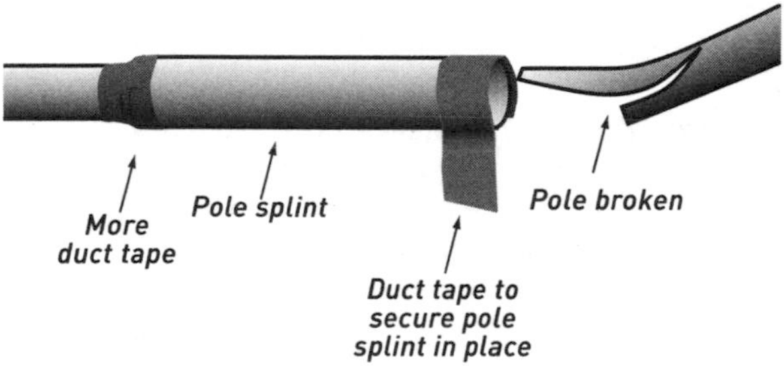

More duct tape   Pole splint   Pole broken

Duct tape to secure pole splint in place

Fig. 5-2. Tent-pole repair sleeve

Repairing a Pole Burr

Burrs or snags typically happen near pole joints (fig. 5-3)—the result of recklessly snapping the sections together rather than fitting each section into place one by one (see An Ounce of

Prevention: Don't Snap!). Inspect your pole joints on a regular basis and smooth any burrs or snags you find. Finally, a use for that file on your pocket tool! Other smoothing devices: a piece of sandpaper, an emery board, or even a flat rock, if you're desperate.

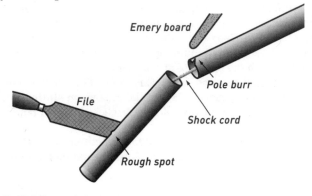

Fig. 5-3 Tent-pole burr

Replacing Broken or Stretched-Out Shock Cord

If you routinely camp in really cold weather or if the shock cord in your tent poles isn't up to snuff, you may someday find that there just isn't enough snap left in the cord to secure all your pole sections together easily. It can be done with a large dose of patience, but who has that when darkness is falling and the wind is kicking up?

If this happens to you, the easiest thing to do is to send the pole(s) to a pro (see the appendix, Repair Facility Reference Guide, at the back of this book) who can rethread them with fresh cord. This operation can be performed at home, but it is rarely worth the headache, and you run the risk of damaging the pole parts even more.

AN OUNCE OF PREVENTION: DON'T SNAP!

It's tempting to just flip your tent poles apart and let the shock cord snap the sections together, but this is one of the most common ways that poles are damaged. The impact on the pole tips results in cracks and splits. Instead, unfold the sections and carefully fit the ends together. When it's time to pack up, separate the pole sections and fold them together, starting at the center of each pole rather than at an end (this minimizes stress on the shock cord).

WATER PROBLEMS

The bad news: Leaks happen. You will, at some point in your camping life, experience some wetness in your tent. Leaks happen for one of the following reasons:

+ Seams are improperly sealed or not sealed at all.
+ Floor material is faulty or worn.
+ The rain fly's waterproofing has worn off.
+ Condensation occurs.

The good news: You can prevent or minimize condensation (see Preventing Condensation, earlier in this chapter), and you can fix all the other causes. After you determine why the tent is leaking (it's not always obvious), chances are that the solution is simple and inexpensive.

Sealing Seams

These days, most good double-wall tents come with factory seam-taped rain flies and floors. When shopping for a tent, look for this key feature, which adds a few bucks to the price tag but is well worth the money. If your tent didn't come sealed (single-walls typically are not taped and must be hand-sealed) or if you just want added protection, buy a good seam sealer and get to work.

Pick a warm, sunny day and set up your tent in the yard with the rain fly inside out. Stake the tent and fly out tautly so the seams are stretched and ready to drink up that sealer. Make sure the seams are clean, then wipe them with a bit of alcohol on a cotton ball to make them more receptive to the sealer.

Paint each and every seam on the fly and around the inside of the tent floor with sealer. For tough-to-reach corners and places where webbing attaches to fabric, apply some sealer with a syringe, injecting it into place.

Be patient and let the sealer dry thoroughly before you pack up the tent and fly, or the fabric will bond to itself—an ugly and unfortunate mess.

For single-walls, the technique is a bit different, yet still simple. Set the tent up and stake it out tightly. Crawl inside and seal all the seams, being sure to reach all the corners and crevices.

TIME-SAVING TIP: If you're leaving on a big trip tomorrow and need your tent seam-sealed today, mix your seam sealer with McNett's Cotol-240, a urethane cure accelerator which speeds cure time up to only two hours.

Repairing Peeling Seam Tape

Even if your tent did come with factory-taped seams, that doesn't mean you're eternally safe from leakage. The tape can eventually start to delaminate. If this happens, simply peel off the remaining tape and give the seams a good cleaning, using isopropyl alcohol. Then apply seam sealer, as described above.

Reviving a Tent Fly's Waterproofing

Has this happened to you? Your rain fly, which used to make water bead up and roll right off, now gets saturated and saggy.

The fly seems to be in good repair otherwise. One possible solution is to reapply waterproofing, or DWR, to the fly.

Set the tent up in your yard on a sunny day and start by giving it a good cleaning (see Cleaning and Storing Your Tent). Then apply a spray-on DWR treatment (ask at your outdoor shop for one specifically designed for tents) as evenly as you can to the exterior of the fly and let it dry completely before repacking. (See Chapter 1, Fabrics, for additional information on spray-on waterproofing.)

If the waterproof coating on the inside of your rain fly starts to peel or flake, you can rejuvenate it the same way as for the tent floor (see below).

Reviving a Tent Floor's Waterproofing

You fall asleep to the pleasant, hypnotic sound of rain drumming on your tent. About four hours later, you wake up because your feet are cold and clammy. No wonder—there's a puddle of water at the bottom of the tent, and your down sleeping bag is a sodden sponge!

Tent floors are subjected to rocks, roots, sticks, and pricks, among other hardships, so it should come as no surprise if your tent floor eventually gives way to a bit of dampness. Especially if the tent is old or inexpensive, it may need a fresh coat of waterproofing to jump-start it back to life. If the floor coating is flaking, peeling, or just plain tired, here's what to do.

First, clean the tent and remove any residual coating by putting the tent in your washing machine. That's right—this is the one time when you are allowed to go this route. As described above in Cleaning and Storing Your Tent, the washer and dryer wreak havoc on the waterproof coatings of your tent. But because you need to strip the old coating in order to replace it, the washing machine is your best bet. Run it through the gentle cycle with cold water and a touch of mild powdered soap (such as Ivory Flakes). Then pop it in the dryer on low heat for about five minutes. Remove the tent and hang it until completely dry. Then scrub the tent floor with a vegetable brush to remove any remaining flakes of waterproof coating. **NOTE:** If the tent has been factory-taped, this process will have started to delaminate the tape. Just peel it off and seam-seal, as described above.

When the tent is clean and dry, set it up. Using a polyurethane product that is designed specifically for the task (check your outdoor shop for the best options), simply follow the instructions and evenly paint the inside of the floor using a foam paintbrush. Let it dry completely before packing it away. **NOTE:** The new coating may make the consistency of the fabric a bit waxier and crinklier, but performance will only be improved.

A Groundsheet Is a Tent's Best Friend

One of the best things you can do to prolong the life of your tent and prevent any floor leakage is to use a groundsheet. Sure, it takes up precious space in your pack, but if the trip promises to be wet or if you are protective of your new investment, you may want to make the trade-off. Many tent makers now offer custom-made groundsheets for a tent of any shape, but these can cost around $50 and weigh much more than a homemade one. Making your own groundsheet will take only a few minutes and cost you less than a fast-food meal.

You'll need a large sheet of waterproof material. There are loads of options: an old vinyl shower curtain, a piece of polyethylene from the hardware store, nylon from a fabric store, even a piece of Tyvek housewrap scavenged from a construction site. (Tyvek is extremely lightweight, but it's not the most durable choice. In fact, it will probably last only a single season.) You'll also need scissors, a marker, some duct tape (of course!), and grommets (optional).

1. Lay the uncut groundsheet out and set up your tent on top of it (without its rain fly and vestibule, if it has one). Stake the tent out tautly.
2. Using the marker, trace the outline of the tent onto the ground sheet.
3. Trim the excess from the groundsheet, following an invisible line two inches inside the line you traced around the tent (fig. 5-4). This is to prevent any overhang which would direct rain underneath your tent floor. This is very important! When trimming is complete, no portion of the groundsheet should extend beyond the footprint of the tent.
   NOTE: If you use nylon (a good choice because of its light weight and durability), cut exactly along the traced line. Then sew a two-inch hem around the perimeter of the groundsheet to prevent the fabric from fraying.

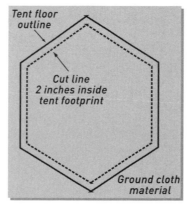

Fig. 5-4. Making a ground cloth

4. (optional) If you plan on using grommets, instead of cutting uniformly two inches inside your tracing, cut the corners right on the line and arc the sides inward two inches. Then attach grommets to the corners. Now you can firmly attach the groundsheet by looping the grommets over the tent-pole tips when you set up the tent. Plus, you can use the groundsheet as a pack cover in the rain, or rig it as a tarp for a cooking shelter or vestibule extender.

DUCT TAPE TIP

If you opt to use a shower curtain, polyethylene, or Tyvek for a groundsheet, cut long strips of duct tape in half lengthwise. Then carefully fold the strips over the edges of the groundsheet. This will protect the edges from tearing or shredding.

REPAIRING HOLES AND TEARS

Whether it's from a flying ember from your campfire or a carelessly packed tent stake, sometimes your tent sustains a wound that needs fixing. There are a number of easy ways to fix it, depending on the size and shape of the injury. (See Chapter 1, Repairing Synthetic Fabrics, Fixing Small Gashes.)

6 SLEEPING BAGS AND PADS

IMAGINE THIS:
You have spent a day's pay on a cushy, inflatable sleeping pad and you're ready to reap the benefits. But after a close encounter with a jagged branch, the mattress of your dreams is fatally wounded with an inch-long gash. Do you have the surgical skills to bring it back to life? Or will you sleep on the cold, hard ground?

Maybe you marched too many miles, labored up too many hills, carried too heavy a load, or dodged too many raindrops. Whatever the reason, sometimes you just need to crawl into a fluffy, cozy cocoon at the end of the day. When the going gets tough, a good sleeping bag and sleeping pad are like a sanctuary.

If you're looking for a great warmth-to-weight ratio, a down sleeping bag is the way to go. Fluffy down plumules also last longer than any synthetic fiber. Synthetic bags are best for

QUALITY COUNTS

When shopping for a bag, crawl inside to check its size. You want plenty of space to squirm, but not too much, because your body has to heat that space. If you camp in cold weather, be sure to have about six inches of extra room at the feet to store your camera, water bottles, and other gear you want to keep dry.

people on a budget or those who often find themselves camping in wet conditions.

The key to a sleeping bag's success is "loft," a term that refers to the bag's thickness and its ability to capture and hold the heat of your body. You are your bag's primary caregiver, and your number-one goal is maintaining this loft. Over the years, a bag will inevitably deflate a bit, but with proper care, a high-quality sleeping bag should last as long as you.

CARING FOR AND STORING DOWN BAGS

The main drawback with down is that if you get it wet, it degenerates into a bunchy mess. Make every effort to keep a down bag from getting wet—like investing in a waterproof stuff sack. If your down filling does get wet and clump up, declump it by gently working the clusters apart with your fingers. Dry the bag and check for more clumps.

Over time, down can shift around inside the bag's baffles (mesh barriers inside your bag that hold the insulation in place), so you'll want to redistribute it. With the bag flat on the ground, simply push the pillowy stuff around inside the bag until it is uniformly distributed.

Never, never, never store your down sleeping bag in its itty-bitty stuff sack for long-term storage! The longer your bag stays compressed, the more fluffiness it will lose. It's fine to use a stuff sack while you're on the trail, but the minute you get home, release it from that confined space, give it a good fluff, and store it in a place where the loft can stay lofty. You can spread it out under your bed, hang it in a closet, or place it in a big, breathable storage bag with a drawstring top. If you don't have a storage sack, use a king-size pillowcase. Store your bag in a cool, dark, and very dry place, such as a basement (if yours is historically dry) or closet.

CARING FOR SYNTHETIC BAGS

Synthetic sleeping bags still provide some insulation when they get damp or wet, whereas down fails miserably. Although it's not exactly blissful to sleep in a wet synthetic bag, it's certainly more pleasant than passing the night in a wet down one.

Synthetic bags' number-one enemy is heat. When drying a synthetic bag in a clothes dryer, be sure to use the lowest possible dryer setting and monitor the drying process.

CLEANING SLEEPING BAGS

Unlike your long johns, your sleeping bag doesn't need to be washed after every trip. You do need to keep the sleeping-bag lining clean, however. Here's what happens: your average grungy outdoorsperson climbs into the sleeping bag with few or no clothes on. Soon the bag's lining is contaminated with bug repellent, sunscreen, trail dust, and body oil. Eventually all that can make its way into the insulation, and loft begins to die a slow death. The moral: Don't sleep naked.

Most bag manufacturers recommend washing a bag after every 20–30 nights of use, unless something really sloppy happens such as a spilled pot of soup or leaky fuel bottle. Before washing, make sure all the zippers and Velcro tabs are closed.

AN OUNCE OF PREVENTION: LINERS

To keep your sleeping bag clean and to avoid having to wash it, use a sleeping-bag liner made of silk, cotton (in summertime), or a synthetic material. Not only do liners keep your bag clean, they're wonderfully comfortable— like slipping in between clean sheets. Unlike a sleeping bag, a liner can be washed after every trip.

If left open, they can abrade delicate linings and coatings.

When you do wash your bag, make a trip to the Laundromat, so you can use jumbo, front-loading washers without an agitator in the center. The agitator in most home washing machines can twist and damage a sleeping bag's insulation fibers and baffle material. Use cold water, the gentle cycle, and a mild, nondetergent soap (found at specialty outdoor shops or natural food stores). Then wash the bag a second time without the soap to remove any lingering suds.

When transferring your bag to a clothes dryer, be careful not to drag or stretch it—you can easily damage the interior baffles. Go for the largest dryer you can find and set it on a cool to medium setting. Check the bag periodically to make sure the fabric isn't scorching hot and the insulation isn't bunching. It may take close to two hours to thoroughly dry a bag, so be patient. Contrary to some popular advice, don't put a tennis ball or sneaker in the dryer with your bag—this can damage the insulation and baffles. You can, however, place clean, dry bath towels in the dryer to suck up some of the moisture. Check the towels periodically and swap wet ones for dry ones.

Or, if it's a warm, sunny day, you can hang your bag lengthwise from a clothesline or lay it flat on a picnic table.

Never dry-clean your sleeping bag. The chemicals wreak havoc on the materials.

AN OUNCE OF PREVENTION: AIRING OUT YOUR BAG

To prevent your bag from getting soggy and losing loft, let it air out each morning on a sunny rock or branch as you break camp. Pack the bag up last. This gives your accumulated body moisture a chance to evaporate.

REPAIRING SLEEPING BAGS

Most field repairs to a sleeping bag involve fabric (see Chapter 1) or zippers (see Chapter 2). One of the best products for repairing the delicate shell fabrics of sleeping bags is Tenacious Tape by McNett. Essentially, it's an instant patch that leaves no sticky residue (like duct tape, alas) when you remove it to make a stitched repair back home.

SELF-INFLATING SLEEPING PADS

If you've never slept on an inflatable mattress, beware. Once you try one, you'll never go back to the old-fashioned closed-cell foam type (unless you decide to use both). The only reason not to carry an inflatable is if you are really trying to pinch some pounds from your load—they're heavier than closed-cell foam pads.

The gist of an inflatable is this: it's either a simple slab of open-celled foam or baffles of some other type of insulative material like down or a synthetic encased in a nylon sheath.

AN OUNCE OF PREVENTION: SAVE YOUR BREATH

Some pads—those with open cell foam in the middle—are "self-inflators." You just open the valve and walk away. When you return, the pad is puffed up and all you have to do is close the valve. Others, like those with down or synthetic insulation inside, require some puffing. Either way, your pad will fare better if you keep the blowing to a minimum. Your breath contains a lot of water, which can build up inside the pad to cause mildew. So unfurl the pad, open it up, and give it some time to puff up on its own. Before bedtime, blow into the valve as needed.

When the valve at one corner is opened, air enters the chamber and puffs the pad up to full capacity (anywhere between ¾ inch for the ultralight pads to three inches for the supercushy ones). Then you just close the valve, and you have a portable mattress. After your snooze, just open the valve again, roll the mattress tight to squeeze out the air, close the valve, and it's a compact bundle ready to pack.

CLOSED-CELL FOAM PADS

Closed-cell foam pads used to be smooth surfaced, but now there are all kinds of ridged designs to provide more comfort. These pads are light and incredibly durable, but they need to be kept away from direct sources of heat so they don't melt. If a closed-cell foam pad gets a tear in it, a little duct tape will mend it. You can cut away damaged portions and use the scraps for other insulating purposes. Here's one idea: Make a backpacking bed for Fido. Cut a pooch-sized square of foam to pack along so your dog doesn't nudge you off your pad in the middle of the night.

DUCT TAPE TIP

Use duct tape and a scrap of closed-cell foam pad to make a water-bottle cozy. Cut a square of foam sized to wrap perfectly around your water bottle, then duct-tape it in place. Slip a bottle of hot soup or cocoa into the cozy after breakfast, and at lunchtime you'll be treated to a warm drink.

CLEANING AND STORING SLEEPING PADS

Like all your precious gear, pads should always be stored clean and dry. When a pad gets grimy, just wipe it down with warm, soapy water, then rinse and air dry. If the valve on an inflatable pad gets gunked up with grit, blast it with a garden hose, then be sure to let the pad dry thoroughly with the valve open.

All pads should be stored flat; self-inflators should go to rest with the valves open. That's because foam has a surprisingly good memory, and might hesitate to puff up if it's rolled into a tight wad for too long.

REPAIRING A LEAK IN A SELF-INFLATING PAD

If your inflatable pad springs a leak in the field, you'd better be ready with the right repair tools, because a gashed inflatable is almost as bad as no pad at all.

Sometimes it's painfully obvious where the leak is; other times, you have to be Sherlock Holmes. If you can't pinpoint the hole by listening for the telltale hiss, submerge the pad in water (either the tub back home or a still pool in the field) and look for air bubbles.

Once you've located the leak, fixing it is a snap if you follow these steps:

1. Clean the problem area with an alcohol cleaning pad from your first-aid kit. Open the valve.
2. Smear a generous gob of Seam Grip into the gash. If it is a small puncture hole, inject the Seam Grip into place using an irrigation syringe.
3. Cut a round patch of Tenacious Tape about ½ inch larger in diameter than the hole, and stick it in place. (If you don't have Tenacious Tape, duct tape will work, but be prepared for a gunky residue when and if you ever peel it off.)

 **STOVES**

IMAGINE THIS:
All day long you've been toiling up Mount Whatsitsname, dreaming about a hot cup of cocoa and a delicious bowl of minestrone soup. When you finally make it to camp, you commence dinner-making, only to find that your stove has a case of the flu—it sputters and coughs and emits only a lukewarm yellow flame. This could be catastrophic! Will you be dining on cold cacciatore for the next few days? Or can you coax your stove back to life and eat like royalty?

Choosing a backpacking stove can be a bewildering affair. At the store you'll undoubtedly be faced with shelves of complex-looking contraptions with metal wires, tubes, valves, and thingamajigs, plus an array of fuel choices that range from variously sized and shaped prefilled metal canisters to fill-it-yourself bottles and one-gallon cans of fuel. There are a number of factors to consider in your stove-buying decision: the terrain and conditions you frequent, your tolerance for

QUALITY COUNTS
It's tempting, but don't use the dregs of that old gallon of white gas that's been sitting in your garage for a couple years. Splurge (five bucks) and buy a fresh can of the stuff each season. It will spare your poor old stove a lot of trouble—clogging, sputtering, and general grumpiness. Always use fresh fuel for the best performance.

fiddling and cleaning, and the types of meals you choose to cook. That said, most good backpacking stoves can be categorized according to fuel type, and they fall into two basic categories: canister-style stoves and liquid fuel burners.

Canister stoves are available in various shapes and sizes, but all contain some blend of pressurized fuels that are released under pressure as burnable gas. Canister stoves tend to be cheap, simple, quiet, and convenient. On the downside, the canisters themselves tend to be more expensive, difficult to recycle, and finicky in truly cold weather. Stoves that run on pressurized canisters will still work down to about freezing, but they require some extra care (see below).

The majority of liquid fuel stoves have detached refillable fuel bottles. (**NOTE:** There are a few exceptions—for example, stoves that burn liquid fuel stored in small, integral tanks below the burner.) Although not as convenient as canister

AN OUNCE OF PREVENTION: PACKING STOVE AND FUEL

Stoves and fuel require a bit of packing precision—you don't want a bent pot support or a leaky fuel bottle to come between you and a hot meal. Some stoves come with nifty padded cases; another good way to ensure protection for your stove is to pack it inside your nesting cookware. (If you use non-stick coated pots, be sure to wrap the stove in a small pack towel or bandanna to prevent scratches on the coating.) Stash detached fuel bottles in an outside pocket of your pack, if possible. If not, double-bag the bottles in hardy zipper-lock bags, then pack them near the bottom of your pack so that if a leak does happen, it won't contaminate all your food and gear.

stoves (they require a pumping mechanism to pressurize the tank and deliver fuel to the burner), liquid fuel stoves are best for colder weather.

Most liquid fuel stoves burn white gas, commonly found in gallon containers under the Coleman name. White gas is the fuel of choice because it packs more BTUs for its weight than other liquid fuels, including automotive gasoline or kerosene. Some stoves, called multifuel stoves, burn a variety of fuels, which is a boon if you are traveling someplace where white gas is unavailable. If given the option, though, always choose white gas, because it burns cleaner and hotter and you'll end up spending less time cleaning your stove. As a rule, stoves that run on white gas perform better in cold weather.

USING CANISTER STOVES

Once a canister stove goes kaput, there is not much you can do to fix it. However, there are a few things you can do to boost the performance of your canister stove and keep it cooking longer.

Bringing Full Fuel Canisters

As you burn fuel, the pressure in the canister decreases, and with it, efficiency. So start each trip with full canisters and save those half-spent ones for warm-weather or car-camping trips.

DUCT TAPE TIP

If your stove runs on prefilled, pressurized canisters, make a custom-sized canister cozy to boost performance in cold weather. From a scrap of closed-cell foam pad, cut a square sized to fit around your canister, then duct-tape it in place. It should not fit so tightly that it cannot be slipped off easily when it's time to change canisters.

Warming the Canisters

As the canisters burn fuel, they get colder and more sluggish. To solve this, you can do a couple of things. First, tape one of those disposable or reusable hand warmers to the bottom of the canister. This helps enormously. Or set the canister in about one inch of water. Warm water works best, but cool water will help as well.

Setting Up a Wind Block

This is a bit different from wrapping a complete windscreen around the burner as you would do with a liquid fuel stove (see below). With a canister stove, in which the fuel tank is attached directly to the burner, a full windscreen can actually generate too much heat, resulting in melted control dials. To create an effective wind block, simply nestle your stove behind a rock or tree, or use pot lids or other items you have on hand. Just be sure there is plenty of ventilation around the burner.

AN OUNCE OF PREVENTION: DON'T FORGET MATCHES

No matter what type of stove you use, remember to have a couple different lighting tools on hand. Lighters work great until your fingers are cold and numb, so play it safe and always pack a box of waterproof matches as a back-up. Two easy ways to waterproof regular wooden matchsticks: dip them in paraffin wax, or paint them with clear nail polish.

USING LIQUID FUEL STOVES

These are more field repairable than canister stoves, which is a big plus. Be sure to read your stove's instruction manual and pack it along with you. Because the mechanics of stoves differ according to brand, much of what you need to know is specific to your model. These manuals provide detailed instructions on how to troubleshoot your particular stove. Entrust the little manual to its own zipper-lock baggie and stow it safely away in your stove storage sack. In a nutshell, that little booklet could save you if you end up having trouble in the field. That said, however, here are a few concepts and tips that are general enough to apply to most liquid fuel stoves.

AN OUNCE OF PREVENTION: CARING FOR YOUR STOVE

Before every trip, give your stove a tune-up. This means disassembling it as much as possible, wiping down all the parts (fig. 7-1), greasing all the O-rings with a silicone lubrication, and checking that you have a well-stocked repair kit to bring into the field with you. Closely inspect all your O-rings to make sure they're in good shape. The rubber should be soft and supple. If not, lubricate the rings with a silicone lubricant. And always be sure to have the appropriate spares in your repair kit.

Priming

It is imperative to know how to properly prime—preheat—your white gas or multifuel stove. (Canister stoves require no priming.) Many people complain that priming is a royal pain largely based on luck, but this just is not the case. Priming may be somewhat of an art, but it is easy to master with a little practice. Just do the practicing at home, not in the field.

Generally, priming entails filling a fuel cup on the bottom of the stove with gas, lighting the fuel, and letting it burn down while the stove heats up. When the gas is mostly burned off

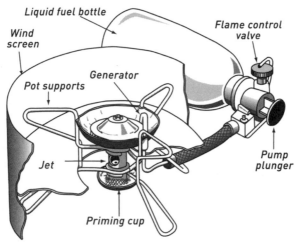

Fig. 7-1. Stove

and the flame is similar to that of a candle, it is time to start the stove. Turn the flame control on, but keep it at a low blue flame for a couple of minutes before cranking it up. If the flame dies out before you're able to ignite it, quickly turn the control knob up a bit and try to relight. Hopefully, the stove will still be warm enough that it will burst to life. If not, or if you're faced with a giant yellow flare-up, let the stove cool down and start all over again. Remember, practice makes perfect.

Cold-Weather Tip
When the weather turns cold, camp stoves inevitably get balky, but you can boost your stove's efficiency and make that hot drink happen a wee bit faster if you use a windscreen. This will drastically improve boil times. If your stove didn't come

with a windscreen, follow these steps to make one out of a piece of aluminum roof flashing from a home improvement store (fig. 7-2).

1. Cut a piece of 10-inch (high) flashing long enough to wrap around your stove and the biggest pot you expect to use.
2. Cut two five-inch slits two inches from each end—one on the top, one on the bottom.
3. Along the bottom edge, cut small wedge-shaped vents every few inches—these act as air vents.
4. When you're ready to use the windscreen, simply wrap it around your cooker and connect the ends via the slits. Secure the two ends with a rubber band or a paper clip.

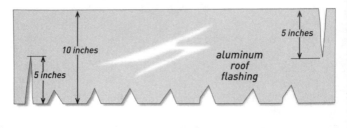

Fig. 7-2. Making a windscreen for your stove

DUCT TAPE TIP

For a more stable stove, cut a square of old closed-cell foam pad sized to fit the base of your backpacking stove. Wrap the foam generously with duct tape for insulation, and you have a stable cooking platform that works great in the snow.

Cleaning the Jet

The jet is a tiny hole inside your stove that transforms the liquid fuel into a burnable fine mist. With normal use this jet becomes clogged with carbon, resulting in a sputtering yellow flame rather than the desired hot, steady, blue one.

Many stoves these days are equipped with an integral jet cleaner, so all you have to do is turn the stove upside down and a small needle cleans out the hole automatically. (If you're in the market for a new stove, look for this feature—it makes life a lot easier.)

If there's not an automatic jet-cleaning feature on your stove, disassemble the generator according to the instruction manual and prick the hole open with a cleaning tool.

Servicing O-Rings

Those little black circular gaskets that appear at various places on your stove and fuel bottle are critical to good performance. If they're cracked, dried out, or otherwise hurting, fuel is apt to start leaking, which is wasteful, causes performance to suffer, and, most importantly, is downright dangerous. If your O-rings' rubber is not soft and supple, lubricate them with something slimy such as saliva, olive oil, or lip balm. Or replace them with the appropriate spares from your repair kit.

Lubricating the Pump Seal

On stoves with detached fuel bottles, the pump assembly is inserted inside the fuel bottle. On stoves with an integral fuel tank, the pump assembly is built into the fuel tank.

You'll know your pump needs some TLC if there is no resistance to speak of when you pump. In this case, unscrew the pump assembly and take a look at the leather pump cup. This little circle of leather needs to remain supple and moist in order to create the desired pressure inside the fuel bottle. If the pump cup is dry, brittle, or cracked, apply some lubrication: olive oil, saliva, or lip balm.

WATER FILTERS

IMAGINE THIS:
You've just marched uphill for four hours and both your water bottles are bone dry. You stop for the night at a lovely lake, whip out your trusty water filter, and commence making potable water. After you have pumped just a few ounces, your filter stages a mutiny. Pumping becomes excruciatingly difficult. Do you stick your head in the lake and start slurping out of desperation, or can you coax your filter back to working order?

There are a number of ways to make water safe to drink. You can boil it, but boiling is not practical for backpackers because it means that you'll have to carry a lot of extra fuel, plus the boiling and cool-down process is time-consuming. However, boiling is the most sure-fire way to remove all pathogens.

Using iodine or chlorine tablets is another option, often favored by seasoned outdoorsfolks because it's weight- and cost-effective. A bottle of iodine costs less than $10, lasts for many trips, and weighs only a few ounces. The main drawbacks with iodine or chlorine are the swimming poolish taste (which can be remedied with a sugary drink mix) and the fact that iodine and chlorine cannot kill tenacious hard-shelled protozoa like *Cryptosporidium*. Also, pregnant women and people with compromised immune systems should not use iodine.

A relatively new water treatment technology is ultraviolet rays. With these light and slender devices, you just clip the stick into the water and click a few buttons. UV zaps the water to cleanliness. Drawbacks: they run on batteries (pack spares!) and they're a bit delicate, so pack them carefully.

Using a water filter or purifier is quick, easy, and safe, which is why so many backpackers carry them. (**NOTE:** The term "water filter" applies to devices that remove protazoa and bacteria; "water purifiers" also remove viruses.) Water filters/purifiers are portable devices that separate the cooties from the water with a few strokes of a pump. They do have a serious drawback, though: they tend to clog, which can be a royal pain when you're thirsty.

Make sure you buy the right device. If you'll be camping with your family of five, opt for a bigger, heavier unit designed to handle a lot of water. If it's just you and the Appalachian Trail, save the ounces and go with a smaller, more packable filter. Make sure the device is designed for your intended use.

Read the label. Be sure it removes *Giardia lamblia* at a minimum. If you're concerned about viruses, look for a purifier that claims to remove them as well.

The best stores have the devices on display that you can fondle, pump, and prod. Play with them. This will give you an idea of how ergonomic it is.

Ask a lot of questions. Talk to salespeople who have used

QUALITY COUNTS

If your filter of choice doesn't come with a prefilter, fork over the extra bucks to get it. Sometimes sold separately, these devices fit on the end of the intake hose to remove the larger chunks of sediment that can clog the filter element. This will save you headaches in the field and also extend the life of your investment.

different units. Inquire about field maintainability, longevity of filter elements, and general word of mouth.

CLEANING AND STORING A WATER FILTER/PURIFIER

Be good to your filter/purifier, and you'll triple or quadruple its life, not to mention help it work more efficiently. They all come with elaborate cleaning/maintenance instructions, which you should follow exactly and carry with you in a zipper-lock bag. Preventive cleaning before and after each trip—especially before long-term storage—is a smart move.

Give it a bleach job. At the beginning and end of the hiking season (at least), pump a solution of one capful of household bleach and one quart of tap water through the filter.

Store it properly. Avoid storing your filter/purifier in a zipper-lock baggie or any other type of nonbreathable sack. Instead, opt for a mesh bag that promotes airflow and ample drying time.

If the pumping becomes difficult, break open the instructions and get to work. Cleaning techniques vary from brand to brand, but some general tips will work for most models.

Backwash it. When output starts to slow, detach the intake hose and attach it to the filter outlet. Then pump away to send a backwash of clean water through the filter, loosening some of the accumulated gunk. After backwashing or before storage, pump a diluted bleach solution through the filter to sanitize it. **NOTE:** Not all models can be backwashed. Check your manual to see if yours can.

Scrub the ceramic element. If your filter element is ceramic, you can drastically improve output by removing the cylinder and scrubbing it with a toothbrush (an old one specifically designated for filter cleaning, not the one you use on your teeth!). After scrubbing, swish the filter around in the water and it's good to go.

USING YOUR FILTER/PURIFIER

Your filter/purifier could mean the difference between being really sick for a couple of days or not. Follow these tips on how to take care of your filter/purifier so it can take care of you.

Handle it carefully. Dropping can cause tiny cracks that let bugs through.

Keep it cozy. In cold weather, don't let residual water inside the filter element freeze up. This can cause it to crack. Be sure to rid the filter of all water when you're done using it. And on cold nights, wrap it in a towel or tee shirt and stow it in your sleeping bag.

Don't be a slave driver. Use your filter only when you need it. For instance, there's no need to filter water that you will boil for spaghetti or hot cocoa.

Use a prefilter. If you need to fashion one on your own, wrap a paper coffee filter or a piece of cotton cloth around the intake hose and secure it with a rubber band.

Start with the cleanest water you can. Don't make your

AN OUNCE OF PREVENTION: CHOOSE YOUR WATER WISELY

If given the choice of filtering your drinking water from a roiling, brown, silty river or a clear pool, you will go with the latter, right? Of course. **TIP:** Poke around and make sure there are no obvious signs of animal activity. In other words, if there is a huge pile of bear poop on the riverbank, head upstream. Of course, there is no guarantee that there is not another bear poop right around the bend, but minimize your exposure to cooties wherever you can. Pumping at or near the water's source is always a good idea.

TROUBLESHOOTING GUIDE TO
WATER FILTERS/PURIFIERS

WHAT HAPPENS		
No water enters the intake hose.	Filter/purifier is extremely difficult to pump.	Water leaks from the plastic filter housing.
WHY IT HAPPENS		
Unit needs to be "primed."	The filter element is clogged.	Usually an O-ring or seal problem.
HOW TO FIX IT		
Varies by brand. Read owner's manual. Don't worry; it is usually a very simple, easy maneuver.	Clean the filter as per the owner's manual (varies by brand).	Disassemble the unit and inspect all all seals. Lubricate with silicone or re-place as needed.
HOW TO PREVENT IT		
All seals need to be airtight so when you pump, it's like a vacuum, sucking up water. Keep it totally free of grit; one tiny grain of Colorado River silt can disrupt a seal.	There is no way to avoid having to clean your filter altogether, but you can extract max-imum efficiency from it by letting water settle before pumping and then using a prefilter.	Keep those O-rings supple with silicone lubrication.

Table 8-1.

filter/purifier work harder than need be. Seek out pools rather than currents, because moving water stirs up sand and debris. Keep the intake hose off the bottom of the lake or riverbed where it tends to suck up sand, mud, muck, leaf detritus, and who knows what else.

Let water settle. Dip up a pot full and set it aside to let the suspended solids settle out. An hour or two helps, but leave water overnight if possible. This simple step gives you cleaner water to process, which can triple the time between cleanings or replacement.

DUCT TAPE TIP

If the intake or output hose springs a leak (a crack or a puncture), wrap it neatly with a few turns of duct tape. Or, if the wound happens near either end of a hose, just detach the hose, snip away the damaged section with scissors or a sharp blade, and reattach the hose to the filter.

 **COOKWARE**

IMAGINE THIS:
You've finally reached camp and commenced the dinner-making process. You have a decadent feast planned for your friends—home-dried Bolognese sauce over fettuccine, and fudge brownies for dessert. When you unpack the cookware, you discover rusty gouges covering the bottom of the trusty nonstick pot that cost you a fortune. Cooking in it won't kill you, but could you have taken better care of your cookware to preserve that all-important nonstick coating? You bet your biscuits!

Cooking pots come in all sorts of shapes, sizes, and materials. To decide what's right for you, consider the types of camp meals you cook, how many you cook for, your threshold for the weight you carry, your durability needs—and, of course, your budget.

Aluminum pots are the most economical, which might explain why Boy Scouts have been relying on them for decades to cook their franks and beans. Aluminum is also quite lightweight, which makes it a good option for backpackers. But, alas, aluminum dents easily, and unless it is coated with a nonstick finish (which boosts the price), it requires some serious elbow grease to clean.

Stainless-steel pots are a bit heavier than aluminum, but they can stand up to years of backcountry abuse. Stainless also has a slicker, easier-to-clean surface, so your macaroni and cheese–tuna surprise will not become one of your pot's permanent features.

Titanium pots pack a hefty price tag, but if you're a true ounce-counter, you may be seduced by their light weight. Titanium is surprisingly strong, but unless it has a nonstick coating, food likes to stick to it, although not quite as much as to uncoated aluminum.

Composite pots are usually built from a thin layer of aluminum on the outside (to trim ounces) and a layer of stainless steel on the inside (to prevent sticking). It is a happy medium, but this type is not as widely available as the others.

Once you have decided on the type of metal that is right for you, consider these features:

+ A nonstick coating makes cleanup way easier.
+ Tight-fitting lids keep heat inside where you want it.
+ Black outer finishes absorb heat faster and boost cooking efficiency.
+ Rounded bottom edges are easier to clean, plus they help heat creep up the pot sides for even distribution.
+ The best way to go is with pot grippers used with plain, handleless pots. Swing or bail handles are usually flimsy and they can heat up quickly, which results in burnt fingers.

QUALITY COUNTS

When shopping for kitchen accessories, go for the stuff labeled "Lexan." It is a sturdy, lightweight, heat-resistant plastic that is ideally suited for camping. For bowls, plates, and cutlery, Lexan is the way to go. You'll also find Lexan cups, but most veteran backpackers prefer insulated, lidded plastic cups (coffee travel mugs) because they keep drinks hotter longer.

CARING FOR YOUR POTS

Nonstick pots bear a pretty hefty price tag, so treat them with respect. Metal can scratch the coating off the bottom of your pot, resulting in rust spots, so opt for plastic or wooden cutlery (not metal) for stirring your soup.

Pack your cookware carefully. That means packing it in the inner, padded sanctum of your pack, not near the bottom where it might get crushed or dented each time you drop your pack.

DUCT TAPE TIP

Want a handy place to store a stash of duct tape? Wrap a healthy length around your water bottle or the handle of your largest utensil (a wooden spoon if you carry one, or even your Lexan fork or eating spoon). When you need some tape, just unravel the proper amount, rip it off, and start repairing—a mini duct-tape dispenser!

CARING FOR YOUR POCKETKNIFE

Learn to take care of your trusty pocketknife, that handy tool that chops your food, spreads your peanut butter, whittles your fire-starting twigs, helps with gear repairs, and opens the cold bottles of beer at trip's end.

When your pocket tool is clean, make sure all the hinges and joints are in good working order by opening and closing them a number of times. If the joints are grabby, apply a drop of cooking oil to the hinges.

Sharpening Your Pocketknife

A dull blade is more than a nuisance, it's downright dangerous. Dull blades tend to skid around the cutting surface, often resulting in cuts where you don't want them (like your hand) rather than where you do (like your onion). Knife sharpening is an art. There are a variety of techniques, but here is the simplest way to stay on the cutting edge:

1. Lubricate a honing stone with water.
2. With the blade positioned at about a 20-degree angle to the stone (fig. 9-1), draw the blade toward you by flicking your wrist. Changing the angle of the blade creates different effects.
3. Flip the knife over and sharpen the other side of the blade, this time working away from your body. Be sure to make the same number of strokes on each side. Do 10 strokes on one side, then 10 on the other, then repeat. The key is to apply steady, even pressure on the stone. Don't push too hard.
4. Test the knife by lightly scraping the blade across your thumbnail. If you've removed a thin layer of nail, your knife is good to go.

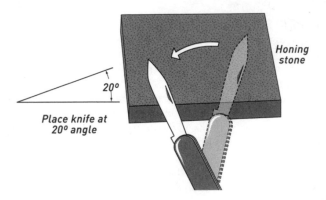

Honing stone

20°

Place knife at 20° angle

Fig. 9-1. Knife sharpening

CLEANING YOUR COOKWARE AND DISHES

If your pots don't have a nonstick coating, you can be much more nonchalant about cleaning them. Pack a steel-wool scouring pad if you want. But nonstick pots, which are increasingly popular, require a bit more TLC, just like those fancy ones in your kitchen at home. Don't use anything abrasive to clean them—no steel-wool pads, just elbow grease and a soft sponge.

Lost your scrubby sponge? Use sand, a pinecone, horsetail, or ashes from the campfire—they make terrific abrasive agents. Just toss a handful into the pot and scrub with your hand or a cloth. Snow also works great in wintertime. **NOTE:** These natural abrasives are safe to use with nonstick pots; just don't overdo it. If you can get away with just a "soft" cleaning, do it.

If you're in charge of dish duty for the night, fill up the biggest pot with water, add a squirt of biodegradable soap if the grease factor is high, heat it up on the stove, then go to it. If there are hard-to-scrub remnants caked on, bring the water to a boil and let it cool till your hands can stand the heat. Warm, soapy water on a chilly night makes dish duty much more bearable. Plus, you walk away with the cleanest hands in camp, which is quite a luxury.

On short trips, leave the soap behind. But on trips of a week or more, grease will build up on your pots and utensils, so pack a small bottle of unscented, biodegradable camp soap.

Never wash dishes directly in a water source. Human food remnants and soap do not belong in a backcountry lake or river. Move at least 200 feet away from the water. If there are a lot of chunks of food left over in the wash pot, filter them out with a bandanna and add them to your trash bag. This is a much better option than dumping remnants on the ground, where critters can find them and, in turn, become conditioned to pester campers for snacks.

When you're doing dishes for a large crew, a lightweight collapsible bucket is great. (This type of bucket also does double duty as a group water hauler, for bringing water up from a river or lake.) Fill the bucket with clean rinse water for that final dip.

CLEANING YOUR POCKETKNIFE

Boil some water and let it cool for about five minutes. Then drop in your knife—with all the elements opened wide—and let it soak for a few minutes. But make sure the water has time to cool off a bit, and don't leave your knife soaking for too long or the plastic casing could melt. Remove the knife and scrub the joints with an old toothbrush to loosen the innermost specks of grime.

A simpler alternative: Put the dirty knife—again, fully opened—into your dishwasher. In the field, try scouring your blade with ashes from the campfire.

AN OUNCE OF PREVENTION: STAYING OUT OF HOT WATER

Need a foolproof dish-duty avoidance tactic? Just confess your hatred of doing dishes, then make good by doing other chores, such as helping with the food preparation, pumping water, or hanging the food bags. There's usually someone in the group who hates doing those things as much as you hate dishes, and who will gladly trade chores.

REPAIRING COOKWARE

The bottom line is that there are not really many ways to field-repair cookware and utensils (these latter are small-ticket items anyway). If one of your cooking pots gets a dent, try gently hammering out the dent at home, using a rubber mallet. Remember to go slow and easy so as not to inflict even more damage on the poor malformed pot.

10 HYDRATION SYSTEMS

IMAGINE THIS:
You're packing up for a long-awaited five-day backpack in your favorite national park. You reach for your hydration bladder and immediately your nose knows that something isn't right. You forgot to drain it and now it's a fifth-grade science experiment—it reeks of mildew. Will you forever be drinking water that tastes like old socks, or can you bring it back from the brink?

We all know the importance of staying hydrated while hiking, and now, lucky for us, we have many different options for carrying and drinking water. There are bottles of all different shapes and sizes, plus hydration systems with camel-like capacities and drinking tubes.

When it comes to water bottles, Lexan—a hard, practically break-proof plastic—is the way to go. It absorbs less odor than traditional plastic bottles, making it a good choice for food storage and rehydration, too.

CLEANING PLASTIC WATER BOTTLES
While Lexan rarely if ever holds a smell, old-school plastic bottles get stinky and/or stained over time. If this happens to you, try mixing a bottle full of water with:

> the juice of one lemon
> a couple tablespoons of baking soda
> a couple tablespoons of white vinegar

After a good long soak, run your bottle through the dishwasher.

If the smell just won't quit, try wrapping up a charcoal briquette in some newspaper. Insert it into the bottle, screw on the cap, and let it sit for a few days. The charcoal will absorb the odor.

If your plastic bottle is stained with red wine, mildew, or anything else, fill it with water and add a couple tablespoons of liquid bleach. Let it sit overnight, then wash it out.

AN OUNCE OF PREVENTION: WATER BOTTLES

When washing any type of plastic bottle in the dishwasher, be sure to place it far away from the heating element (usually below the bottom rack) so it won't melt.

STORING WATER BOTTLES

Always store your bottles with the caps off to promote air circulation and prevent mildew and odor buildup.

CLEANING HYDRATION SYSTEMS

With their plasticky reservoirs and long, skinny drinking tubes, hydration systems aren't as simple to clean as water bottles. But it's not rocket science either. There are a number of cleaning systems, tools, and tablets on the market, which are easy to use and not too expensive, but you can easily fashion your own cleaning kit if you prefer.

There are two types of reservoirs on the market today: those with screw-top closures and those with wide-mouth closures (zip-top or Velcro). To keep your screw top from leaking, make sure it's free of debris, which can gunk up the gasket and cause a leak. Periodically clean the threads with a toothbrush and water. If you're having trouble getting your zip-top bladder to close, lubricate the grooves with Vaseline or olive oil—it should then snap right into place. The Velcro closures should be cleaned regularly, too. (See Caring for Synthetic Fabrics, Chapter 1.)

To wash out a hydration system, fill the bladder and hose it with warm water and add two tablespoons of unscented liquid chlorine bleach. Shake well and let it soak overnight. If you have a small-diameter, long-handled brush (a gun barrel brush works well), scrub out the hose. Then rinse well and dry, using one of the DIY dryers, described below.

Removing Odors and Flavors from Hydration Bladders

Combine about ½ cup baking soda with about two cups of water (increase this ratio for larger bladders). Pour the mixture into the bladder and shake well. Next, add ½ cup of lemon juice and shake. After about 10 minutes the bubbles will subside. Vent out the gas, cap it, and let it sit for about ½ hour. Lastly, rinse a few times with hot water and dry completely.

AN OUNCE OF PREVENTION: HYDRATION SYSTEMS

To prevent mildew and unappetizing smells and flavors from plaguing your hydration system, be sure to empty and dry it completely before storage. Never leave a full or partially full bladder at room temperature for more than a day or two. You can, however, store a filled system in your fridge indefinitely, because cooties won't grow in the colder air.

Making a Hydration System Dryer

As described above, air drying your system is essential, but can be tricky because the soft sides of the bladder collapse and stick together. But here are two contraptions you can make in a snap to ensure your system is dried and stored properly.

For screw-top reservoirs (fig. 10-1):

1. Saw off one of the short sides of a plastic clothes hanger.
2. Wrap a bit of duct tape around each exposed end to prevent damage to the bladder.

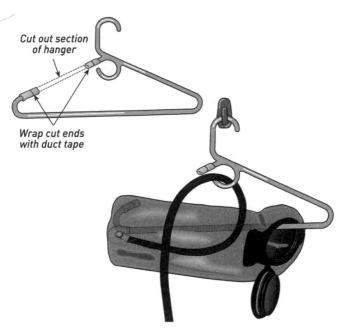

Fig. 10-1. Drying a screw-top bladder using a coat hanger

3. Simply insert the long bottom edge into the bladder and hang it up! This props open the mouth enough to allow airflow.
   For wide-mouth reservoirs (fig. 10-2):
1. You know those wire hangers you get from the dry cleaner with the cardboard cylinders along the bottom? Remove the cardboard and snip off a four-inch section.

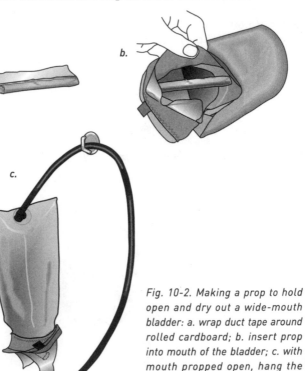

Fig. 10-2. Making a prop to hold open and dry out a wide-mouth bladder: a. wrap duct tape around rolled cardboard; b. insert prop into mouth of the bladder; c. with mouth propped open, hang the bladder to dry.

2. Wrap the section in duct tape, to prevent it from getting wet.

3. Then, just insert the piece into the mouth of the bladder crosswise, so that it props it open. Hang the bladder upside down by the hose and let it dry completely before storing.

DUCT TAPE TIP

Fix a split or hole in your drinking tube with a quick turn of duct tape.

REPAIRING HYDRATION SYSTEMS

Chances are, you'll want to replace your bladder and hose assembly every couple of years, just like you replace water bottles. But there are two common yet easy-to-fix problems that might crop up before that time comes.

Fixing a Puncture or Hole in a Bladder

Wipe the wounded area with an alcohol pad to clean it. Once dry, dab a bit of Seam Grip into the hole. Cover it with a rounded patch of duct tape. (Remember: Rounded patches are

AN OUNCE OF PREVENTION

Sometimes, during the course of wrestling your bladder and tube in and out of a full pack, the hose may pop free from the bladder, a very unfortunate mess that can ruin your day. To prevent this from ever happening, simply pop the tube off, apply Superglue to the inside threads, and stick it back on. Now they are forever joined, till death do they part.

far less likely to peel than square ones.) Let it dry—preferably overnight—before filling.

Securing a Loose Bite Valve

If the connection between bite valve and hose is loose, you might get an annoying drip. Remove the bite valve and snip off a ½-inch section of the hose. Replace the bite valve and secure it with a plastic zip tie from the hardware store if necessary. A good practice: After each drink, blow water back into the hose. This can prevent bite valve drips and also keeps the hose from freezing in colder weather.

APPENDIXES

A. 50 FIXES WITH SEAM GRIP

You've read about Seam Grip a number of times in this book. It's one of the most versatile repair tools you can buy—as a liquid stitcher, adhesive, sealer, and protectant. For inspiration, here are over 50 different ways you can put a tube of Seam Grip to good use!

- ✦ Seal seams on tents, tent flies, tarps, and awnings
- ✦ Repair rips, tears, and holes in tents, tent flies, tarps, and awnings
- ✦ Coat high-abrasion areas on tents, tarps, and awnings
- ✦ Repair damaged stitching on tents, tarps, and awnings
- ✦ Reattach fasteners and guy lines to tents, tarps, and awnings
- ✦ Reattach shock cords to tent pole interiors
- ✦ Reattach tent pole tips
- ✦ Repair ripped zippers on tents
- ✦ Seal the seams on all types of raingear
- ✦ Repair rips and tears in rainwear and other breathable waterproof clothing
- ✦ Repair leaks in self-inflating mattresses
- ✦ Cement valves in self-inflating mattresses
- ✦ Create a non-slip surface on top of inflatable mattresses and sleeping pads
- ✦ Repair valves and punctures in inflatable mattresses, balls, toys, etc.
- ✦ Repair Hypalon, PVC, and vinyl inflatable watercraft

+ Create an abrasion layer to the bottoms of inflatable watercraft hulls
+ Seal seams and repair rips and holes in all types of dry bags
+ Repair shoe and boot seams
+ Rebuild worn shoe and boot soles
+ Repair delaminated soles and insoles
+ Repair cracks and fill holes in shoes and boots
+ Waterproof seams on shoes and boots
+ Reattach climbing shoe rands
+ Seal ends of shoelaces
+ Repair rips and tears and seal seams on backpacks
+ Reinforce high-abrasion areas in backpacks
+ Lock screws and threaded fasteners in place and seal out moisture
+ Prevent knots from coming untied
+ Prevent lines, ropes, webbing, and threads from unraveling
+ Prevent cut fabric from unraveling
+ Repair rips and tears in garments
+ Repair torn zipper skirts
+ Repair rips and tears in sleeping bags
+ Repair seams on all types of gloves
+ Repair holes in all types of gloves
+ Coat glove palms to create added grip and to prevent abrasion
+ Coat bottom strap of snow gaiters to prevent abrasion
+ Seal leaky ice chests
+ Repair and seal the seams on fishing waders
+ Repair damaged and delaminated fishing boots and soles
+ Repair and seal the seams on dry suits, wet suits, and accessories
+ Repair sunshowers, bladders, and valves

+ Repair emergency flotation/rescue devices
+ Repair survival suits
+ Repair life vests
+ Repair kayak spray skirts
+ Repair and seal boat covers, awnings, upholstery, and decking
+ Seal and caulk boats
+ Coat cast iron and other metal fittings to prevent rust
+ Repair orthopedic supports
+ Repair rubber tires
+ Repair broken knobs on camping stoves
+ Create non-skid pads for stove legs
+ Repair eyeglasses, goggles, and protective eyewear
+ Repair delaminated skis

B. REPAIR FACILITY REFERENCE GUIDE

When the repair task seems too daunting or you just want the pros to handle it, try one of these well-respected repair shops.

Boulder Mountain Repair—bags, packs, tents, clothing
641 South Broadway
Boulder, CO 80305
(303) 499-3634

Dave Page, Cobbler—boots
3509 Evanston Avenue North
Seattle, WA 98103
(800) 252-1229
www.davepagecobbler.com

The Grant Boys—bags, packs, tents, stoves, lights, clothing
1750 Newport Boulevard
Costa Mesa, CA 92627
(949) 645-3400
www.grantboys.com

Kelso Camping and Repairs—bags, tents, clothing
P.O. Box 2714
Anaheim, CA 92804
(714) 827-7527
www.kelsocover.com

Rainy Pass Repair, Inc.—bags, packs, tents, clothing
5307 Roosevelt Way Northeast
Seattle, WA 98105
(800) 747-7867
www.rainypass.com

Stitchlines—bags, packs, tents, clothing
3750 South Broadway
Englewood, CO 80110
(303) 781-9044

Sunshine Tent Pole Specialists—tent poles
23679 Calabasas Road, Suite 162
Calabasas, CA 91302
(818) 222-5217

TA Enterprises—tent poles
8212 Northeast 99th Circle
Vancouver, WA 98662
(800) 266-9527
www.polesforyou.com

Tent Repair Services—bags, packs, tents, clothing
20½ Sea Street
Camden, ME 04843
(207) 236-0997
tentrepair@acadia.net

ZRK Enterprises—bags, packs, tents
279 Palm Avenue, Suite 1
Ashland, OR 97520
(800) 735-4620
www.zipperrescue.com

THE MOUNTAINEERS, founded in 1906, is a nonprofit outdoor activity and conservation club, whose mission is "to explore, study, preserve, and enjoy the natural beauty of the outdoors...." Based in Seattle, Washington, the club is now one of the largest such organizations in the United States, with seven branches throughout Washington State.

The Mountaineers sponsors both classes and year-round outdoor activities in the Pacific Northwest, which include hiking, mountain climbing, ski-touring, snowshoeing, bicycling, camping, kayaking and canoeing, nature study, sailing, and adventure travel. The club's conservation division supports environmental causes through educational activities, sponsoring legislation, and presenting informational programs. All club activities are led by skilled, experienced volunteers, who are dedicated to promoting safe and responsible enjoyment and preservation of the outdoors.

If you would like to participate in these organized outdoor activities or the club's programs, consider a membership in The Mountaineers. For information and an application, write or call The Mountaineers, Club Headquarters, 7700 Sand Point Way NE, Seattle, WA 98115; 206-521-6001.

THE MOUNTAINEERS BOOKS, an active, nonprofit publishing program of the club, produces guidebooks, instructional texts, historical works, natural history guides, and works on environmental conservation. All books produced by The Mountaineers Books fulfill the club's mission.

Send or call for our catalog of more than 500 outdoor titles:

The Mountaineers Books
1001 SW Klickitat Way, Suite 201
Seattle, WA 98134
800-553-4453
mbooks@mountaineersbooks.org
www.mountaineersbooks.org

The Mountaineers Books is proud to be a corporate sponsor of Leave No Trace, whose mission is to promote and inspire responsible outdoor recreation through education, research, and partnerships. The Leave No Trace program is focused specifically on human-powered (nonmotorized) recreation.

Leave No Trace strives to educate visitors about the nature of their recreational impacts, as well as offer techniques to prevent and minimize such impacts. Leave No Trace is best understood as an educational and ethical program, not as a set of rules and regulations.

For more information, visit *www.LNT.org*, or call 800-332-4100.

OTHER TITLES YOU MIGHT ENJOY FROM
THE MOUNTAINEERS BOOKS